MY JOURNEY OF CHALLENGE, FAITH & TRIUMPH

MY JOURNEY OF CHALLENGE, FAITH & TRIUMPH

BUT WHAT A RIDE!

LEON WELLINGTON

Leon Wellington
My journey of challenge, faith & triumph

Published by Spines
ISBN: 979-8-89383-300-3

CONTENTS

ABOUT THE AUTHOR

I was born in a small community in Southern Manchester, Jamaica, called Asia, and attended the Frankfield Primary School, a government public school governed by the Methodist Church. I was fortunate to be "home-schooled" by my mother, who operated a basic school at our home where other preschool children of the community would attend.

Growing up in this rural village, life was routine. There were animals to attend and find them good pastures that would keep them for the day. Then, there was water to fetch from a tank on our property — enough to fill a large copper jar, and, as I recall, it would take 16 of my containers to fill. What a blessing it would be when it rained.

My public school days were as normal as one could expect. I had many classroom teachers who knew me well and tried to keep me in line, partly because they knew my mother. I tried to be a good student, as it would not be to my benefit if negative news about my behavior ever reached home. That behavior had a different characteristic when I left the school compound, as some evening conflicts ended in classmates going home with bloody noses and bruises from fistfights.

In my very rural community, my life revolved around home, school, and church. This was my environment until I succeeded in the first, second, and third Jamaica Local Examinations. I pay tribute to my primary school principal, Clinton C Lewis, who tutored me free of cost for all three local examinations. This success gave me my first opportunity to earn a wage. I moved to Clarendon, an adjoining parish, to work as a pre-trained teacher at the Mitchell Town Primary School, where my cousin Charles Logan was principal. While my environment still revolved around home, school, and church, my horizons began to expand as I formed new relationships.

After two years at this school, I received an invitation from hometown friends, Robert Kennedy and Luther Preddie, to visit Canada, where there was the possibility of a better future and furthering my education. I gladly moved to Toronto, but within the year I returned to Jamaica as my immigration status was unsettled, and I had no desire to be an undocumented alien in any foreign country. I returned to work in the civil service and later the insurance industry. The experience of living in Canada briefly was of tremendous value and a life-changing event. It helped me develop broader perspectives and relationships, and set better priorities, and later, it was the country that helped me achieve my academic objectives.

Upon my return to Asia, I became once more involved in church life, and it was then that this unfulfilled, unsatisfied feeling to achieve more became very intense. I realized that satisfying this desire could only be achieved by becoming academically prepared. My then-church pastor, Kenneth G Vaz, encouraged my congregation to appoint me as an ordained youth elder, and when that was finally done, my life was never the same.

After a series of events that came in quick succession, within two weeks, I was registering for my first semester as a ministerial student, and the rest, as they say, is history. Looking back, I am convinced that the Lord was leading my life from those very early days.

Since graduating in June 1977, I have gone on to do a Master's in Public Health degree at Loma Linda University. I have served the church in the capacity of district pastor, youth, health, temperance, family life, and development director, conference secretary, conference president in the Central Jamaica Conference, and West Indies Union secretary and president.

Now, I'm a proud retiree of the Inter-American Division, where I served as Vice President, Communication Director, and ASI Secretary.

In 2003, the Government of Jamaica awarded me the Order of Distinction, Commander Class, for services rendered to religion in Jamaica.

I am also co-founder and president of the Educational Foundation for Children's Care Inc., a charitable organization established to care for abandoned, abused, neglected, and homeless children in Jamaica. We now operate the Alta Vista Children's Village in Four Paths, Clarendon, before we move to Bog Walk in St Catherine.

In 2021, I received the Marquis Who's Who in

America Distinguished Humanitarian Award for my philanthropic work.

Jamaica: A Brief History of its People and Culture

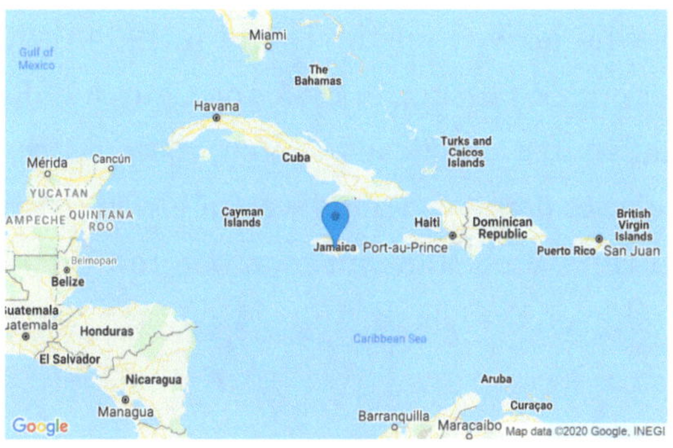

Let me introduce you to a country once considered the "pearl of the Caribbean." Located just 90 miles to the south of Cuba, the largest Island in the Caribbean, Jamaica is the third largest Caribbean Island whose early inhabitants were Arawak natives. When Christopher Columbus arrived on the island in 1494, he found peaceful people who were descendants of the Tianos. They had settled here from Brazil, in South America, around 1000 BC, and called the land Xayamica, meaning *"Land of wood and water."* Upon his arrival, Columbus proceeded to claim the land for Spain. The Spanish colonialists proved to be very brutal in their treatment of the natives, to the extent that within a few decades after Columbus' death, almost all Arawaks were exterminated.

Spain held the island under its control and fought off many buccaneer raids on St. Jago-de-la-Vega, its main city now called Spanish Town. Eventually, England claimed the island in a raid, though the Spanish did not relinquish their claim to the island until 1670.

Jamaica's first encounter with Christianity came in the form of Roman Catholicism, introduced by **Spanish settlers** who arrived on the island in 1504. When the British captured Jamaica in 1655, the Church of England (later called the Anglican Church) became the state church. Other denominations were allowed to function, and over time, Protestantism soon outgrew the Catholic membership on the Island.

Port Royal

Once known as the 'Wickedest City on Earth,' Port Royal, located on the southeastern Palisados Peninsula of the island, was one of the largest towns in the English colonies during the late 17th century. It became a base of operations for buccaneers, including Captain Henry Morgan, because of its excellent strategic location in the middle of the Caribbean and between the Americas. From Port Royal, these buccaneers preyed upon and plundered the heavily laden treasure fleets departing from the Spanish Main. In return, these buccaneers kept the other colonial powers from attacking the island. Africans were captured, kidnapped, and forced into slavery to work on plantations when sugarcane became the most important export on the island.

After 1670, the importance of Port Royal and Jamaica to England increased significantly due to trade in slaves, sugar, and raw materials. It soon became the mercantile center of the Caribbean area, with vast amounts of goods flowing in and out of the port through an expansive trade network. It was known worldwide as a port where every imaginable evil was practiced.

Unfortunately, the glory of Port Royal was short-lived. On the morning of June 7th, 1692, a massive earthquake hit Jamaica. The tremors rocked the sandy peninsula on which the town was built, causing buildings to slide and disappear beneath the sea. An estimated 2000 Port Royalists were killed immediately in the disaster, and many more perished from injuries and disease in the following days. Many people still feel that it was a direct divine intervention and judgment upon a city known for its practice of wickedness.

Many slaves arrived in Jamaica via the Atlantic slave trade during the same time enslaved Africans arrived in North America. During this time, there were many racial tensions, and Jamaica had one of the highest instances of slave uprisings of any Caribbean Island. Most famous was the Morant Bay Rebellion led by Paul Bogle in 1865. After the British crown abolished slavery in 1834, the Jamaicans began working toward independence, which they achieved on August 6, 1962. [1]

Religion has been a part of life in Jamaica from its very early days. It hosts a wide variety of religious expressions. Although more than 60% of its population subscribes to Christianity, many other religious organizations, such as Judaism, Hinduism, Buddhism, and Islam, enjoy peaceful coexistence. Jamaica has even given birth to its own religion called Rastafarianism.

With more churches per square mile than any other country in the world, it is easy to see why many regard Jamaica as a Christian society. Our island is home to multiple denominations; Roman Catholic, Anglican, Baptist, Presbyterian, Pentecostal, Seventh Day Adventist, Moravian, Methodist, and an assortment of Pentecostal and Church of God congregations, being just a few that can be found here. While Jamaica's Christian roots hail from Europe, several other forms of Christianity that are also practiced locally are strongly marked by African influences, namely Kumina, Pocomania, Zion, and the Ethiopian Orthodox Church.

Most Jamaicans are Protestant. The largest denominations are the Seventh-day Adventist and Pentecostal churches; a smaller but still significant number of religious adherents belong to various denominations using the name Church of God.

Seventh-day Adventism and its place in Jamaican history

Seventh-day Adventism was not one of the early entrants in Jamaica, having arrived only in 1891, but it has had a huge impact on the nation of Jamaica. Several factors have contributed to this, as summarized by Dr. Bertram Melbourne in an article on Jamaica published **in the Encyclopedia of Seventh-day Adventists:**

1. The fact that one in nine Jamaicans is Adventist.[94]
2. The success of Northern Caribbean University and the positive contribution of its graduates to nation-building.
3. The impact of Adventist Christian education through our educational institutions; (d) the impact and presence of the Adventist Development and Relief Agency (ADRA), which participates in disaster relief efforts

(community development by providing water for some communities, toilets in rural Jamaica, etc.).

4. The involvement and positive influence of its members as employees in government ministries and agencies, as well as in corporate entities.

5. The proliferation of Adventist congregations on the island, in the cities, as well as in remote communities.

6. The contributions to developing the community and nation from church leaders serving on government boards, statutory bodies, and private sector organizations.

7. The positive impact of SDA pastors and leaders preaching on radio and TV stations.

8. The Northern Caribbean University Radio Station's consistently high national ranking. Furthermore, the Ministry of Education signed an agreement for the church's Pathfinder Club program/curriculum to be offered in the national school system to benefit all students.

9. Presently, the Chaplain of the Jamaica Constabulary Force is Dr Gary Bhudoo-Fletcher is an ordained Seventh day Adventist pastor.

INTRODUCTION

The volume you are about to explore will unfold to you many interesting events and experiences from the journey through life that God has guided me over the years. You will encounter many individuals to whom I owe much for assisting to make the journey clearer and possible.

I consider my life and ministry a tremendous success, not necessarily because of what I have accomplished, but because of what God has accomplished through me. Also fully appreciating the fact that the circumstances of my birth and early development would not, under normal circumstances, hold out the prospect of much success. Whatever contribution I have made to the growth, development, and spread of the gospel during my active years, was possible only because I said yes to God's call and the fulfillment of His promise to me.

I must thank the many friends and members who encouraged me to tell my story. Even though I resisted for a while, I was forced to change my perspective because of what God did for us in restoring my wife Shirnet after she became seriously ill, following our retirement from full-time denominational service in 2017. This book is, for the most part, a biography that extolls God's leading in my life. But more so, it is a testimony of how God miraculously restored my wife from a clinical diagnosis of early dementia to the place where we are once again enjoying each other's companionship and fellowship along with family and friends.

When you read her story, you will agree with me that the God who performed many marvelous miracles in Bible times, that still capture our attention and wonder, is still mightily at work in our time, of which I am a witness and beneficiary.

1

BACK TO BASICS

THE EARLY YEARS

During the decade in which I was launched into this world as a babe, most children would begin their journey in life with a struggle that was destined to be "a battle and a march." Some would have to struggle a little harder than others, but to make a success of life, each one's destiny would be achieved through struggle. Many times, that destiny remains unclear or unknown for a while. However, it was generally perceived that before us there was an ever-expanding horizon of possibilities if we would embrace the educational path as our only way up. In especially rural communities, this academic embrace would be our surest route to escaping failure. How many of these possibilities we would be able to achieve or even access, would largely depend upon how motivated one is to change one's circumstances or his/her thirst or desire for success.

From a biblical standpoint, **Jeremiah 29:11** assures us that God's plan for us is to prosper, and not to impair the prospects of anyone. It is comforting, and certainly a boost to self-worth, for one to know that, regardless of the circumstances of our birth, we are not here by accident, but as part of a divine plan.

I was born to a single mother in a quaint little district called Asia, in South Manchester, Jamaica. In those years, it was a deep rural countryside; with no running water, no electricity, and no inside sanitary conveniences, and if, while driving through the district, you blinked your eyes for too long, you might have passed it without noticing. When I was a kid and we heard a motor vehicle coming in the distance or saw the dust in the air behind the vehicle swirling up from the unpaved roads, especially as children we would rush to the roadside just to see it drive by.

I grew up for most of these early years with my grandparents, James and Wilhelmina Sparks. They were poor farmers who decided to take me in their charge so that my mother, Ruth Sparks, could refocus her life, which she did by opening an infant/basic school at home. I still remember being part of that school. I was told that there was just one little problem with having me as a pupil: I could not distinguish between Ruth the teacher and Ruth the mother during school time! (Well, why should I anyway!?)

In my community, at that time, life was centered around three institutions: home, school, and church. My family were members of the Asia Seventh-day Adventist Church and was also among the early

Advent believers in that congregation, so I was exposed to church life very early. Those in my situation would be in "Adventist parlance," known as "Born in the message." The church became, for many of us as youngsters, a vital part of our lives, because it gave us the opportunity to develop public speaking gifts, memory dexterity, musical appreciation, and good social development, as well as instilled in us values and attitudes that helped to successfully guide us through life. Despite the challenges we faced growing up, I am still grateful for this community that cradled me. I feel and understand the words of the Scottish Poet Sir. Walter Scott, who penned the words which say:

> Breathes there the man, with soul so dead,
> Who never to himself hath said,
> This is my own, my native land!
> Whose heart hath ne'er within him burned,
> As home his footsteps he hath turned,
> From wondering on a foreign strand!
> If such there breathe, go, mark him well;
> For him, no minstrel raptures swell;
> High though his titles, proud his name,
> Boundless his wealth as wish can claim;
> Despite those titles, power, and pelf,
> The wretch, concentered all in self,
> Living, shall forfeit fair renown,
> And doubly dying, shall go down.
> To the vile dust, from whence he sprung,
> Unwept, un-honored, and unsung.

GROWING UP YEARS

Growing up in Asia, life was routine. Morning worship was the first engagement, then it was time to take care of the domestic animals and fetch water from a tank to fill a large copper receptacle for daily domestic use before I could go off to school. Most mornings, a visit to the post office was thrown in as well, before I could leave for school, which was a few miles away, in the opposite direction from the post office, and there was no bus, taxi, or Uber to help. Even if there was, we could not afford the cost, so "Zephyr2" had to be engaged at a brisk rate of speed. On those days, should anyone arrive at school after the scheduled 9:00 am start, one could likely meet the principal waiting under the poinciana tree with his "leather enforcer" to urge punctuality. My creative mind decided to write an excuse note to the principal stating, "Please excuse Leon for coming late as he had to wait for the Post Office to open at 8:00 am to collect the mail," to which my grandmother's purported signature was affixed. I was not thinking of the morality of that deed then, what I knew then was that it worked. My justification was that prayer would take care of that deception!

I spent all my primary school years at the Frankfield Primary School in South Manchester, with an eccentric but brilliant principal, Mr. Clinton C Lewis. It was under his principalship and tutoring that I was able to succeed in passing the first, second, and third Jamaica local exams. For those who didn't experience those exams, they were not the easiest to pass. Why? Because one has to be successful in all eight subjects to secure a passing grade for this exam. Fail one of these subjects, and one would need to take the entire eight subjects all over again the following year. That is why, after failing at my first exposure, I couldn't afford to fail another year, so in three years I was done and should be ready to move on to High School.

But there was one problem: I had little financial support, as the Basic School's earnings of my mother were not enough to stretch that far. And yes, there was an absent father who lived in England and had not made contact with us in years. So, the next option was to find a job, earn some money, and support myself; that's precisely what I did. So off I went to Clarendon, a neighboring parish, to work as a pre-trained teacher at the Mitchell Town Primary School. The principal, Mr Charles Logan, a cousin of mine, and his wife were very accommodating in helping me settle, this being my first time leaving home.

These were great days, living and learning a lot, forming new linkages in the community and also at the Lionel Town Seventh-day Adventist Church, which served me well later in life.

This part of the country was one of the largest sugar-producing regions of Jamaica. There were never-ending stretches of sugar cane plantations that provided employment for thousands of families from Clarendon and neighboring parishes. This was a completely new way of life from what I was accustomed to in Manchester because, though both parishes were agricultural, it was a vastly different agricultural production. While Manchester produced a variety of fruit trees, root crops and cattle, sheep, and goats, Clarendon's main production was sugar cane. After spending 3 years in Clarendon, I resigned from my teaching job and decided to explore better prospects by taking an extended summer vacation in Toronto, Canada. This visit opened up a new world of possibilities for me. Some of my friends who were there encouraged me to remain in Canada, but when I applied to do so, my application was refused. It was then, after four months, that I decided to return to Jamaica and not stay beyond my welcome because it was contrary to my principles to remain illegally in any country.

I went back to Jamaica and returned to teaching at the Bethabara Primary School, in New Port Manchester. I had such a great experience with staff and students, but I also determined that teaching was not going to be my profession. It is still gratifying for me to see some of my former students making significant contributions to all areas of life in Jamaica and elsewhere.

The economic realities of life then dictated that I continue working to sustain myself. The desire to grow academically was still strong, but I could not see a clear path to achieving it if I did not continue to earn a salary. What was clear to me was that my path to academic success would not be the traditional one.

I was now ready for a change in career projection, so I decided to explore other possibilities. I applied for an advertised position to become a statistical enumerator with the Government Department of Statistics in Kingston. I was accepted for the job, given the necessary training, and began my new career in the civil service, which was officially noted in the Jamaica Gazette. This brought another dimension of growth since this was a job that required much travel in and to my assigned area of Northern Clarendon. Since I was now eligible for travel assistance and per diem, I was able to purchase my first car, which did give me, as it would to any other youngster, a sense of accomplishment. With this reality, the prospect of college was receding in the distance, or so I thought. The push was now for me to establish a base and build capital for myself. So, I bought my first lot of land in the Marley Mount development in Old Harbor, St Catherine, Jamaica.

After a few years at the Department of Statistics, it was time to move on to another career that offered the prospect of much higher wages. I then moved to explore the Life Insurance industry as a sales agent. My economic stability and growth were now being strengthened by the very good salary that I was now earning every two weeks in this new job. A young man with a car and a good job, what's next? Yes, you're right, look around for the right person to spend the rest of your life with. I was now on that journey, and it was a really exciting journey, so let me tell you about it.

YES, GOD CHOSE HER FOR ME

Well, despite what this subtopic implies, it was not that easy or quick to achieve. I was always involved in church life. My ability to be mobile gave me the opportunity to visit many places and events outside of my locality. But this was not my first time looking around, because as an idealistic young man, I was always keeping a keen eye out for that lucky lady who captured my imagination of what life could be, should we decide to link our lives together in marriage.

I had established beforehand what my parameters of search would be in order to limit my search. One such was that anyone with whom I develop a relationship must share my philosophy of life, as well as my religious beliefs. It would be a big enough challenge to bring someone into my life, who grew up with different family traditions, values, and personal idiosyncrasies, to add to that the complications of a differing religious philosophy. My desire was to find someone who would advance my faith in God and not diminish it. So, rather than limiting myself to my local congregation, (this is not to say there were none at home who qualified, but there was a desire to have a new experience), I would go to events and places where other young people who fit my profile were more likely to be found. One such place was the annual youth camp held by my church organization.

It was now time to pack and go off for a week to mix and mingle with young people from all over the Conference territory. The camp director was none other than one of my favorite pastors, who was to figure prominently in my life in the future, Pastor Lee Herbert Fletcher. My first camping experience was a real awakening. We were placed in units of 8 persons, and each of us was responsible for the welfare of the other, as also camp duties were to be performed on a unit basis. The strict discipline, time-bound activities, and regulated lights out were in sharp, contrast to my lifestyle, but by the end of the week, so much of that was imprinted in my DNA. This youth camp was held at the Discovery Bay primary school, just adjacent to the world's famous and beautiful Puerto Seco Beach in St Ann, Jamaica, which, as campers, we used for our scheduled swim time each day.

Before the week had ended, I had also met one Shirnet Clarke, who possibly came to the camp with the same objective of finding someone with whom she could develop a permanent relationship. After "line call," it was time for breakfast, lunch, and dinner, and there she was, offering to help me get my meals. I was not about to deny such kindness, but that also meant that we would sit together and discover more about each other. One of my questions to her was, "Why are you so interested in helping me?" Her answer was, "That song you sang for devotion, you put so much of yourself in it, it just kept ringing in my ears." I was only doing what I had always done in my home church, and when asked, I chose to sing the song "Lead Me Oh Lord, Lead Me." Was choosing this song a providential choice? I don't know, but she never let me forget that song.

As a unit of boys, one would not be surprised to learn that, as we got used to knowing each other, we would use the time between lights out and falling asleep to talk about any and every subject. There was one young man in my unit, who will remain nameless, whom I discovered was from her parish and knew Shirnet well. So, I proceeded to ask him about this very precocious young lady. My innocent questions, without giving away any hint of interest, or so I thought, were answered quite honestly, I thought. I still remember he concluded by saying, "I wish you luck!" So, I asked Shirnet how well she knew him, and I found out she knew him very well. Before breaking camp, I realized why he said to me, "I wish you luck." He had been trying for a long time, but without success, to be her special friend. She had shown no interest in his direction, so I guess I was the lucky guy. This young man remains our friend to this day. He even got married before we did, and who was asked to toast him at his wedding? Shirnet, indeed. And she did it well, because he was, and still is indeed, a genuinely wonderful person. I guess one has to get that gut feeling, coupled with the divine direction and approval before one can say yes to any proposal.

As the saying goes, "The rest is history." Shirnet and I learned a lot about each other, and as camp was now about to break, we determined that we would continue to communicate, and we did.

I discovered that she was a trained teacher, and was also in her first year of pursuing a bachelor's degree in Education at the University of the West Indies. I learned also that she had seven brothers and two sisters. A rather large family, while for me, I had two brothers, but we never lived together, except for one brother, Val, with whom I had lived at our paternal grandmother's home for only one year. The family dynamics were different and completely opposite. How would I fit in? I quickly realized that not only was it necessary and helpful to share the same religious philosophy, but there were other questions to be answered and adjustments to be made.

Reintroduced to the table of my thoughts was the question of whether to continue building equity or pursue higher education to match my aspiring academic companion. Why did this university student decided to say yes to a youngster with minimum academic preparation at the time? What did she see? While I do not have an adequate answer to that question, I am firmly convinced that this was another instance in which God demonstrated the fact that He continues to guide my life by making this significant life choice for me.

The other three years of her academic pursuit would be time enough to settle that question. We were engaged about one year and a half after meeting, but we had also agreed that completing her education was the priority at this time.

The reason academic concerns became a preoccupation was because of a previous relationship that died. While I lived in Clarendon, attending the Lionel Town congregation, I became interested in someone I thought would be the one with whom I would share my life as a partner. Things were going well until she decided to pursue her educational path and went off to College. The lines of communication after a while became cooler and less frequent, and then cold. My suspicion was that she didn't see a future with this young man, who was bright, but to her, not academically compatible. That relationship ended, and I was on the market again.

WEDDING BELLS

Shirnet's graduation was held in the month of May 1971, and the date we previously decided to be the day we said "I do" to each other, December 19, 1971, was now approaching. The option to go off to college was now not an option I could immediately consider, because it was time to take on the unknown realities of establishing a home, and later a family. The need to keep on working was stark! With great excitement and anticipation, we pressed ahead with our plans. To choose whom we would ask to be our pastoral counselors and marriage officers was an easy choice. Pastor Lee Herbert Fletcher, the Union Youth Director and camp director, Pastor Kenneth C Henry (Pastor KC), Conference Youth Director, and Pastor Roy Ashmeade, pastor of the North Street Seventh-day Adventist Church, who was Shirnet's pastor while she attended Mico college. The North Street Church was also the Church we decided to be the venue for our wedding ceremony.

Shirnet completed her bachelor's degree, graduating with second-class honors, in May 1971, and, on December 19 of that same year, we were ready to take on the challenge of leaving home for good to establish a home of our own. So, in the presence of excited family members and adoring friends, we got married on a beautiful Sunday afternoon at the famous North Street Seventh-day Adventist Church, in Kingston, Jamaica, and then repaired to the home of a wonderful Sister of the Greenwich Town congregation by the name of Sister Whittingham for the reception.

Leon & Shirnet Wellington on their wedding day
December 19, 1971

Signing the register with (L-R) Esmie McLeod,
Pastors Roy Ashmeade, Kenneth Henry and Lee H
Fletcher, looking on.

This was the launch of a new phase of life and adventure, and neither of us had a clue what the future portended. One thing we knew was this: regardless of what the future holds, we would do everything in our power to make a success of our lives together. Many more marriages would succeed today if the parties exercised more commitment and resolve. They would do well to recognize that marriage is not merely a contract, nor is it a contest, but should be a lifelong commitment.

Your mate and you have many different expectations, emotional needs, values, dreams, weaknesses, and strengths. You are two unique individuals, children of the same God who have decided to share a life together. Neither one of you is perfect, but you are and can be perfect for each other. Bring out the best in each other by always seeing to the welfare of the other person. Compliment and compromise with each other, but do not compete, compare, or control.

In 2021, we celebrated our golden wedding anniversary, and credit is all to the providential hand of God leading in our lives, and a willingness to make the necessary compromise. It was not just *"And they lived happily ever after,"* but these fifty years have been quite a journey; and what a ride it has been! This journey that Shirnet has agreed to take with me I would not trade for anything else, as she has been my inspiration, my partner, and my friend, and I am better for it.

THE EXPANDING FAMILY

Since we were a young, struggling couple, we had no funds to buy or build a house for a while, so we started by renting a small two-bedroom house that fitted well in our household economy. We felt proud and excited to be in a home in which we were our own bosses! It did not take us long to settle into a routine of work, home, and church. We had a prenuptial understanding of how we would handle our financial matters, and who would be responsible for what, and this was working well. As time went by, and after a period of adjustment of about two years, we had come to the point where we were comfortable with ourselves and it was time to grow the family and see what our progeny would be like.

The first pregnancy was a really steep learning curve for both of us. It was a time of excitement, but also of challenge and fear. This pregnancy was not going to be one of those trouble-free ones. As the pregnancy progressed, we discovered that Shirnet was experiencing pre-eclampsia. This condition occurs in about 5-8 percent of pregnancies, manifesting after the 20th week, and is characterized by high blood pressure and signs that another organ system, most often the liver and kidneys, may not be working normally[1].

This was not good news, but with the help of our general practitioner, we were able to go to full term. There were, however, some concerns, as the baby's movements became less and less vigorous. The doctors and hospitals did not have the array of diagnostic tools and equipment available as it is today. So, there was another problem to solve; where would we choose to have the baby delivered since there was this challenge? Shirnet, being a graduate of the University of the West Indies, opted for familiar surroundings with friends who were nurses. I agreed because I believed they would be the best equipped on the island.

The long-anticipated day arrived and, with all the preparations done to receive the expected newborn, we journeyed to the hospital. The admission was done, and then all the emotions of anxiety, nervousness, excitement, and joy captured my entire being.

Within twenty-four hours, this feeling of excited anticipation was to change to one of despair! The tense period of waiting ended when the doctor emerged to tell us that his greatest fear was confirmed, the experience ended in a stillbirth as the fetus had died.

DARK DAYS

The following days and months were indeed dark, gloomy, and dreary as we sought to navigate the mountain of disappointment that confronted us. Our plans, our hopes, and our anticipation were all dashed against the wall of despair as we returned home empty-handed. Soon, I discovered that I could not sustain this despair and help Shirnet emerge from her depression. I learned that as difficult as it was, I had to be strong for her. I had to find ways of giving empathetic support and hope, rather than dwell with her on the plane of self-pity. So, words of assurance, encouragement, and prayer, family, friends, and church members were tools convenient and frequently used to help us restore and heal the emotions.

My wife was so discouraged that she thought she would never even try again to give birth after such a disappointing experience. After a while, it was her mother, Bernice Wright, who encouraged and finally convinced her not to give up, for only by trying again would she really "forget" this experience and move forward with life.

It is very vital to build valuable relationships as we journey in this world. Relationships that are not only social in nature but a genuine, personal, and spiritual connection with our Divine Creator; one that we can call upon in our difficult times of crisis and need. It was those relationships that we formed along the way the ones that helped us back to wholeness at a time when we needed them most.

In two years, healing had taken place, and we were ready to try for number two, as we had agreed before marriage that we were going to have four children in our family. Once again, our hopes were lifted when it was confirmed that number two was on the way. Once more, we started to plot the path to receive our newborn. We were encouraged as this time the pregnancy was not as difficult as the first. Emotions were once again raised high as we lived in great anticipation of our little baby girl. We found the daintiest name we could create and, bingo! Let's call her Marvette. We made many trips to Kingston, the capital city, to a gynecologist of renown, in hopes that our fortune would be better this time than the first. All seemed to be going well, and soon it would be time for delivery. We made the usual preparations and off we went to the University Hospital once again. The usual tide of emotions flowed as we waited anxiously for the arrival of the gynecologist, who was scheduled to do the delivery.

Apparently, the baby was ready to be delivered before he could arrive, so permission was given to someone else to proceed. This time, our precious, eagerly anticipated baby girl was born. But, it turned out to be a bitter-sweet moment. We were informed that during the birthing process, the doctors experienced some difficulties, and employed the use of a vacuum extraction device to assist them, but in the process severely damaged the head of the baby. This damage was not repairable and therefore, we would be having a baby girl with severely impaired movements who may never walk, talk, and grow up as a normal child.

This was more than enough trial for a young family to really question God, and we did! The only redeeming factor was that this time, we had a baby to take home. In many ways, that was a form of consolation as we tried to deal with this crisis. We grew to love our baby daughter and gave her the best opportunity we could for eleven and a half years.

There are many couples who give mothers-in-law bad reviews, and doubtless, there may be some who deserve the rebuke. But for me, no praise was too great to give my mother-in-law, who greatly helped us to weather this turbulence. Finally, we agreed to her request to care for our daughter so that we could recoup our lives. This was a blessing for us, and we will remain eternally grateful to Bernice Wright, who now rests in sleep until the resurrection.

All of us come to times in our lives when the clouds hang very low. We wonder if God is really there and if he really cares! There is a song by William J Gaither/Lilly Isaacs that we found rather consoling in our grief, that I will share for your encouragement when you face your time of distress or confusion. Yours may not come in the form ours came, but as long as we are here on this planet, we should all anticipate mountain and valley experiences.

Does Jesus Care?

Does Jesus care when my heart is pained
Too deeply for mirth or song,
As the burdens press, and the cares distress,
And the way grows weary and long?

Cho: Oh, yes, He cares, I know He cares,
His heart is touched with my grief;
When the days are weary, the long nights dreary,
I know my Savior cares.
Does Jesus care when my way is dark
With a nameless dread and fear?
As the daylight fades into deep night shades,
Does He care enough to be near?

Does Jesus care when I've tried and failed
To resist some temptation strong;
When for my deep grief there is no relief,
Though my tears flow all the night long?

Does Jesus care when I've said "goodbye"
To the dearest on earth to me,
And my sad heart aches till it nearly breaks—
Is it ought to Him? Does He see?[2]

So, yes, after eleven and a half years, we had to lay our cherished little Marvette to rest, and we look forward to the great reunion which is part of our Christian hope. Oh! Yes, He cares!

When your clouds of distress hang low, when there are events in your life that confuse you and for which you find no answers, just trust God's omniscience because He has the full scope of your life. To be able to trust Him in the dark moments, you must make your acquaintance in the light, or when things are going well. The prophet Isaiah implores us to do just that; don't wait until you are in the crisis to make peace with your God.

"Seek ye the Lord while he may be found, call ye upon him while he is near: Let the wicked forsake his way, and the unrighteous man his thoughts: and let him return unto the Lord, and he will have mercy upon him; and to our God, for he will abundantly pardon. For my thoughts are not your thoughts, neither are your ways my ways, saith the Lord. For as the heavens are higher than the earth, so are my ways higher than your ways, and my thoughts than your thoughts." Isaiah 55:6-9 KJV

With such episodes of devastating disappointments, you would probably think we would give up trying. Well, it doesn't mean we didn't consider that option, but once again, our wonderful, thoughtful, and forever blessed mother-in-law was the prime mover. Her scheme to take care of our daughter was her way of saying: as long as you keep focusing on Marvette, you would not want to keep trying to overcome this mountain in your lives. She was indeed a visionary and wise woman, from whose wisdom and encouragement we went on to fulfill our prenuptial agreement to fill our quiver with four children.

Although the first two experiences could now be considered as a misadventure, today we are blessed with two wonderful, accomplished, successful sons who, along with their families, have made us truly proud and blessed. The first, Rohann, is now a Pastor with administrative responsibilities, a Communication Specialist, holds a Doctor of Ministry degree, and serves also as a Chaplain & Captain of the United States Air Force.

Our second son, Handel, has his first degree in Aviation, serving as airline Captain for world-class airlines, and flying the largest passenger and cargo carriers, such as the 777 at Qatar Airways and 747 at UPS Airways. He has also qualified himself in the legal field as a Juris Doctor (JD) attorney.

These sons of ours have also made us truly proud of their choice of life's companions. They brought us two wonderful daughters whom we consider replacement for those two we lost. They have also given us great, wonderful, smart, and beautiful grandchildren who have made our lives satisfying and worthwhile.

What if we had given up because of the discouragements and disappointments we faced earlier? I believe we would still be looking back on those disappointments and probably blaming ourselves and others. Today, we look back and thank God even for the lessons learned from those disappointments. We recognize that we can use them to encourage and strengthen the faith of others, and hopefully including you, to trust in the providence of a loving and caring God who says: *"For I know the plans I have for you, declares the Lord, plans to prosper you and not to harm you, plans to give you hope and a future." Jeremiah 29:11 (NIV)*

It was Job who, after experiencing many reversals and crises in life, even the loss of all his children, said *"Though He slay me, yet will I trust Him." Job 13:15.*

That is what it means to truly trust, and if we follow this biblical example, we will truly grow in grace, faith, and trust day by day. Try it!

2

MY PROFESSIONAL JOURNEY

Coming as I am from a poor and what some would consider an unpromising background, with little financial support, the prospect of achieving any kind of success was not impossible, but rather remote. One only has to look at the success, or lack of it, that some of my classmates have made of their lives. If one was to escape the low expectations of many, life was destined to be a gigantic struggle. Many who were in more fortunate circumstances than myself have not made it beyond primary school.

My community was not one of those to which people would gravitate, except for the teacher, police-man, postmistress, or other such government employees who were assigned or posted in their jobs there. It was one of those communities that you instinctively know that, when you reach your senior teenage years or early adult life, you should work your way out. That too was my trajectory. Somehow, I was determined that my fate would be different; how much different, I don't know, but I didn't like what I saw around me.

MY NON-TRADITIONAL PATH TO ACADEMIC FULFILLMENT

What I came to understand early was that, if I were to make a success in life, a good education would be my golden key. But, as I mentioned earlier, there was not the parental support that was necessary. So, I was determined not to be the average "Joe" in my community, but to try every means possible to succeed in life. I tried farming, but that didn't work out. Next, I took the job of delivering the telegrams from the local post office, since in those days no one knew what cell phones, WhatsApp, or texting were. Those electronic means of communication were not even thought of. By becoming a courier for the communities around carrying telegrams from the post office to their homes, I would soon get enough funds to purchase and maintain my first bicycle and take care of other personal needs.

There were some colleagues who unknowingly became my motivators along the way. Because I believe they deserve mention here, I will highlight two of those.

The first was my cousin, Whitford Shaw, whose circumstances were not very different from mine. He showed great industry in trying to earn funds by selling individual copies of the New Testament books of Matthew, Mark, Luke, and John. I remember that well because I remember helping him to sell some of these testaments. I did not know how financially rewarding it was, but what I know is this: not long after that, he left our community to live in Montego Bay. He continued selling books, and soon he was attending high school and later college. He finished his degree in Theology and went on to serve in the pastoral ministry and saw denominational service in England, Canada, and all over the United States.

The second was my very close friend and primary schoolmate, D. Robert Kennedy. Our friendship was a little strange, though, because there is no other primary schoolmate I can recall with whom I had so many physical fights, as I had with my friend. Looking back, I suppose I was somewhat more aggressive than he was. Several evenings he would be going home with many scars and busted lips as a testament to another day's scuffles! And predictable, once he got home, both he and his mom would be coming over to make the justified complaints and seek redress. We would be strongly urged to make peace, and so we did, even if somewhat reluctantly. But there was something notable about my friend; I could expect him to call me in the morning so we could both journey together to school. We would sit together at the same school desk, which was built for two students. We studied together all the way through the grades and local exams. Interestingly, when we took the First Jamaica Local, we failed it together. I guess that became a motivator, and in the next three years, we successfully progressed through the First, Second, and Third Jamaica Local Exams.

Our time in primary school had now ended, and the time had come to make the big decision: What's next for us? I was quite open to a journey with him, but his choice of profession was the determining factor that caused us to travel on separate tracts. He decided to go on to college to pursue the ministerial course, and I knew definitely that that was not going to be my choice. I could not fathom why he would want to become a pastor, which was not a very payable job. Furthermore, I did not see ministerial characteristics in my friend. I jokingly said to him, "The first time you come to preach at this church, I will take up my hat and leave!" My determination, as I told him, was to be the best layperson I could be, but to follow him to the ministry, no, not my "Cup of tea!" At the time appointed, off he went to college, and off I went to begin earning some cash for myself to lay my foundation and become a financial success. That was when I decided to go off to Mitchell Town, in Clarendon, to begin life as a pre-trained teacher in grade 4 (PT4), for which I was now qualified.

Interestingly, when he first came back from college to preach at our home church, I was there to welcome him. He asked why I didn't leave as promised, and my answer to him was that I did not own a hat then! My friend has gone on to achieve several terminal degrees, being a very successful pastor, lecturer, and prolific author. He too has seen denominational service as a university lecturer, and Pastor in Jamaica, Canada, and all over the United States of America.

JOB SEARCH AND JOB SATISFACTION

Settling in Clarendon, my first time away from home, was intriguing, which I also viewed as my best opportunity then to see life from a totally new perspective. It was time to meet new friends, develop my independence, test my personal value system, and, in general, spread my wings. I learned a lot and developed new friends and associations, many of which have lasted a lifetime. So, my first job was to teach junior grades at the Mitchell Town Primary School, in a very rural part of Clarendon. Life was so different from what I was accustomed to, but interesting. The soil was a type of clay that would stick to your shoes whenever it rains, as opposed to the red bauxite earth I grew up on. The clay soil became home to thousands of land crabs at a certain time of year. I was so intrigued to see cars and truckloads of people coming in at night with make-shift torches to search for crabs. Since I wasn't accustomed to seeing crabs in Manchester where I grew up, nor did I eat crabs and was mortally afraid of those two menacing claws, I was able to view all this from the comfort of my windows. My orientation into the teaching profession was adequate, the environment was conducive, and the staff relationship was excellent.

Another new experience for me was riding my bicycle through those "avenues" in the cane fields to the nearest township of Lionel Town; that could be a real struggle. If one should encounter strong headwinds in those avenues, I found it to be a more desirable thing to dismount and push the bicycle, than trying to pedal my way through. But, ah, what a relief on the return journey! Effortlessly, with those tailwinds, I could ride my bicycle with little or no pedaling, and complete the journey in half the time!

After three years, it was time to move on. This move took me to Toronto, Canada, which I found to be a most desirable place to live and work. But my sojourn in Canada was brief, as described earlier in Chapter 1, and I returned to Jamaica and the teaching profession. Although the environment and fellowship were great, and my students were excited and overall anxious to learn, I instinctively knew then that teaching would not be my chosen profession for life. So, in search of a new challenge, I applied for a position in Jamaica's Civil Service and was later offered a position as a Statistical Enumerator with the Department of Statistics. This offered better wage compensation and greater flexibility in time management. After spending about three years in the Civil Service, it was time to move on again. I liked what I was doing, but somehow it did not bring me the personal satisfaction that I would expect from a job. Then I moved on into the Life Insurance industry, which was far more financially rewarding. Although I was enjoying a reasonably good life for a young man with a professional wife by his side, somehow deep down there was that desire for greater fulfillment that none of these jobs I had undertaken so far had offered me. If there would come a time when this job was no longer there, what would my options be? How would I sustain my family? These were indeed perplexing questions for which I found no clear answers.

I continued to serve my local congregation as Youth Leader and Pathfinder Director for several years, ably assisted by my lifelong friend, Ezra Fider, who qualifies as my "brother." We sought to give as much positive guidance by precept and example to the young people, who I believe were positively influenced by our leadership. This I know gave me a lot of satisfaction, and helped greatly in developing my own leadership skills as we interacted with the youth in a personal way. Not only did I serve at the local level in youth ministry, but concurrently served at the Parish level as president of the Manchester Federation of Adventist Youth Societies. It was my privilege, joy, and delight to serve along with some of the greatest, committed, dedicated youth leaders in the parish, many of whom later became lifelong friends.

We executed many youth initiatives through our zone or district Federation days, Pathfinder Club Exhibitions and prizegiving, craft competitions, Youth camps, and street marches, all of which kept our youth in the parish very active and engaged. We experienced great success in holding large quarterly Federation Rallies by bringing together the youth from the pastoral districts for fellowship, worship, and investiture of those completing the requirements for their respective pathfinder courses. Our team represented all the pastoral circuits of the parish and was a large, united, highly motivated cadre of youth leaders. While I will not be able to name them all, my debt of gratitude goes out to Ezra Fider, Daphnie Daley, Percival Simpson, Festus Lewis, Phyllis Lunan, Catherine Morgan, Ethlyn

Morgan, just to name a few as representatives of the whole.

These activities undertaken would generally involve leaders of our church administrations, especially those who served in the youth department, as well as the Youth Ministry of the National Government. Many times, our activities were captured and broadcast on the nightly television news, which made our young people very proud of their clubs and that their stories were being told.

SAYING YES TO GOD'S CALL: DAYS OF PERPLEXITY

It was in the midst of all this beehive of activity, that my local church pastor, Dr. Kenneth Vaz, determined with the local church board that because I had served the local church so well, and the youth on a wider scale, it was desirable that I was ordained as a "Local Elder" in the Church. I had no objections and was grateful that my church appreciated the services that I, along with others, were making to uplift our young people.

It was in the month of August 1973, following the ending of a series of public evangelistic meetings that this ordination took place under the same evangelistic tent.

Amazingly, what I thought would be the final event in the drama, turned out to be just the beginning. That ordination service was so impactful on me, that I became very mentally and emotionally disturbed, enough to tell myself, "I need to do more!" What more could I do?

As my wife and I drove home that Saturday night, we reflected on the events of the day and what it meant for us. Her thoughts were very favorable, but when I told her that I felt the Lord was calling me to do something more, the tone changed. "What more?" "Well, I just feel impressed that the Lord was calling me to prepare for full-time work in the gospel ministry!"

Wow! I knew that the last thing she would want was to be married to a minister. I was surprised by her response simply because I knew that her respect for the ministry was severely damaged because of the attitude of a certain pastor who seemed not to have appreciated her approach to how she dealt with some matters at the church. My wife is not one to keep silent in the face of injustice or what she sees as wrong actions, which sometimes brings her into situations of conflict, and such was the case with this pastor, which made her decide never to marry one. So, having recovered from dealing with the experience of that fallout, she did not easily gravitate to pastors. That for her was bad enough, but now having the prospect of living with one could be really horrendous!

The ensuing discussion was intense. Not adverse, but more of a "what if" situation, how would we manage it? As I recall, upon reaching home, I parked the car on the outside of the house and we engaged in discussion until about 1:30 am before we entered the house!

I recall to this day my wife's response to the question

I posed: "What do you think I should do about this feeling that God is calling me into Ministry?" After a moment of reflective thought, she said, "If that is what you feel the Lord is calling you to do, I will not stand in your way."

It was a shock to me, because if she had said otherwise, I would not have been surprised, and I could pass on this one since my wife would not be comfortable being married to a pastor!

But no, she said yes, and there I was, more perplexed than ever, not because she gave me the "green light," but because of what was going to happen to us during these 4 years that I would be unemployed. How would our bills be paid? How would our car be maintained? She would have to cover all the household and other bills. To this, she committed, and the way was now clear. What I now find really interesting is that the way ahead is not any clearer than it was years before. But here I was, contemplating college, and most of all, a profession I had previously said was "not my cup of tea!" The days following were certainly confusing, as torrents of thoughts flooded my mind with no clearly visible answers.

THE DECISION OF A LIFETIME

Two days later, I was on my way to work and stopped at a gas station in Mandeville to purchase petrol for the journey. While pumping petrol into my car, who came to the other side of the fuel pump? The president of the West Indies College, now Northern Caribbean University, Dr. Lee Herbert Fletcher, whom I knew very well. As a matter of fact, he was previously my Union Youth Director and marriage officer. After the normal pleasant greetings, his next question to me was, "When are you coming to college?" It was not the first time he was encouraging me to improve my academic level by coming to college, but this time the significance of that question was striking to me. What coincidence could possibly bring us together for him to ask a question such as this!? Could this be another divine confirmation of the call? I quickly pulled him aside and away from the fuel pump, and then I related to him my tempestuous weekend! He listened graciously, and when I was through, his "command" to me was, "Go right now to the Registrar's office, tell Aunt Lus, (Lucille Walters) to give you the necessary application forms, and make arrangements for you to take the special entrance test. This should be done as urgently as possible as the College was to open for the first semester in about three weeks. I obeyed and by the end of the day, I had everything in place. Thursday, I attended the entrance exams, which was necessary since I was out of the formal school system for so long. By the following Monday, I was informed that I was successful in the exams and therefore should make plans for early matriculation. Everything was now moving on steroid, with adjustments to be made at home and on the job to arrange for part-time rather than full-time employment.

That was not easy because, when I went to discuss the matter with the Manager, his response was, "Why? You're making good money and you're talking about going to school to come back to make money." I did not tell him I was about to go in to do ministry because I would have played straight into his hands with that argument. I was one of the top-performing agents at the time so, to appease him, we settled for part-time, as I would need the money anyhow to pay my fees. That was only to last for a few weeks, as I soon realized that with the volume of school work, and my being out of the classroom mode for a long time, working part-time would not be a helpful option. I had to make the fateful decision to terminate my employment and focus on one thing: study.

In the meantime, I matriculated for the course, and two weeks after taking that examination I was coming to the first day of classes. Believe me, I had a lot of questions for myself! How did I get here? Am I really sitting in a class preparing for a lifetime of service in the gospel ministry? I had to convince myself that yes, it was really real! It was at this point I said to God: "You know this was not my idea, but You have brought me here, so it's all yours from here on. Help my wife cope, you help me pay my school fees, and You have got to carry me through. If you will do this, then I'm all in!" Having made the decision and now starting my tertiary academic journey, one would have thought I would be sharing the good news with my friend Robert. Not at all. I could not muster the courage to tell him about this "U" turn that I had made.

This was the most difficult decision I have ever had to make up to this point. But, even now I can declare that, outside of deciding who to marry, this was the best decision I ever made in my life: Saying yes to God's call.

Although I did not understand how things would turn out, I knew one cannot go wrong in saying yes to God's divine call and claim on one's life. God's providence will never lead you to any place His grace cannot keep you.

The main challenge for me at college was to ensure I earned the college fees each semester, and there were eight of those. But God was always faithful and true to me and to His promise. Every semester, I was able to find the necessary resources by using the summer breaks to find some profitable employment wherever I could. Real Estate, becoming a Colporteur (selling religious books) and, during the school year, I would do on-campus work in the office at the College Bakery. I was able to return to Canada for two of those summers to sell religious books and magazines in order to earn my scholarship. God was good in that for those two summers and I earned enough money to pay for the year's tuition at West Indies College.

For a long time, I could not tell Robert about the decision I had made. He eventually heard and, when we next met, he was most supportive of my decision, but could not let me off without challenging me by saying; **"You can run, but you cannot hide from God!"**

The longest journey always has an end, so, after four years of "beating the books," I was now approaching the time for graduation! At West Indies College, graduation is not a one-day event, but a whole weekend. So, on the weekend of June 3-5, 1977, the celebrations began that

Friday evening. Like any other graduate, I was excited and grateful. Grateful to God for carrying me through eight semesters of serious classwork, and also grateful to my wife for her encouragement and support. Not only did He take me through successfully, but when I visited the finance office of the institution to reconcile my account, I discovered I had completed the year with a decent credit instead of a debt to be cleared!

I am also grateful to my wife, Shirnet, who largely shouldered the domestic expenses of the home for the entire duration of my study. There were so many things for which we were grateful, including taking us successfully through the loss of our daughter Marvette.

The final march began with the majestic sound of the instruments as they played "Pomp and Circumstances" on Sunday, June 5 at 11:00 am, and, in the presence of family and friends, soon I was striding across the platform to receive my certificate. At about 2:30 pm it was all over, and a new phase of life was about to start for me.

3

THE JOURNEY CONTINUES IN CENTRAL JAMAICA CONFERENCE

EARLY YEARS IN MINISTRY

Graduating from college was much like leaving home for the first time. Now I will have to transition from student life to becoming a worker in the church. What would life be like? During the final semester, the officers of the Central Jamaica Conference, to whom I had applied for employment, came to campus to interview those who had applied. I was confident that I would be selected since God had "arrested" me four years earlier, while I was engaged in what I considered a secure job and placed me in college; I believed with all my heart that He had a purpose for me to fulfill.

I was right, as I was later informed by my conference that my application was successful, and therefore should visit the office for interview and orientation. The interview went well and my new assignment was to become a ministerial intern in the May Pen district of Churches beginning July 1, 1977. Things moved rather quickly, as I had to find a house and relocate to the church district. It was not difficult to find a house as I was directed to a member of the church, Lucille Christian, who would assist greatly by renting me one of her houses.

One of the things about which I had failed to question the conference treasurer was what I should expect as a salary at the end of the month. One of the things I knew was that my conference was not one of the wealthy ones; as a matter, they were having serious financial challenges at the time. I didn't want anyone to get the impression that the salary was any great motivation for coming into ministry.

We set up our home in May Pen and began to do ministry under the supervision of Pastor Edwin Hyatt, who was serving as the president of the Conference at the time. At the end of the month, it was time to collect my first check and the surprise was great and memorable! Would you believe my salary after one month was the equivalent of one week's salary I was earning four years before? I could not immediately share that news with my wife except to say I was not the bigger earner in the household at that time. I was consoled by the fact that there were others in my situation, or who started at a salary lower than mine, and had survived and had done well. I was sure that God would sustain my little family, and never see us go hungry or be in need.

I soon discovered that my sojourn in May Pen was to be a brief one. The administration had taken into consideration my experience before ministry, having served in the local church as a Local Elder, Youth leader, Pathfinder director, and Parish Youth Federation President. I had no way of knowing then that through these assignments God was preparing me for greater service, as He would later dictate. Now in retrospect, I can see how God led in my life, even when I thought I was running away from Him. God is so amazing, and I sometimes imagine what God was thinking and doing when I thought so much that I was in control.

After three months of orientation in ministry, the Conference committee saw fit to appoint me to my first pastoral district, the Chapelton Circuit in northern Clarendon, with continued supervision from the office in Spanish Town. This meant consulting with the President regarding any unusual challenge I might face in the district. Chapelton was a rural township in the hills of Clarendon, a parish which I came to love so much. This part of the Island, I believe, is still one of the most beautiful parts of the country with the hills of Chapelton, Leicesterfield, Smithfield, Blackwoods, the valleys of Pennants, Bryant's Hill, Frankfield, and the great Rio Minho river that flows through the valley from north to south. It was a fruitful parish, and the members were so generous with their produce that I had more than enough to share with neighbors and others.

The pastoral circuit then comprised eight congregations which would cover the entire northern part of the parish. It was very convenient for us as my wife was able to secure employment as a lecturer at the renowned Clarendon College in the township of Chapelton. It was here that my ministry matured, blossomed, and grew. There were several challenges, but thank God we were able to surmount them and grow the churches by adding annually over one hundred new members. Evangelism was not easy for several reasons. Customs diehard in this part of the country, and even if the citizens didn't attend church, they were more traditionalist/nominal Christians. I relate one experience that for me was a "teachable moment," and it stands out in my ministry. The Pennants congregation was the smallest of the eight congregations I had then. Among its members was a short, small-bodied, elderly gentleman by the name of Brother Rumble. He lived a few miles away from the church, up in the mountains, and was the only Adventist member in the area. One day, I had a very pleasant visit with him at home and listened to him tell me a very interesting story about his struggles with the authorities and subsequent imprisonment because of his advocacy for fairness and justice for the sugar workers. The names of his compatriots in the struggle were now prominent trade unionists and government officials, not the least of which was the then Governor General, The Honorable Sir Florizel Glasspole. He told me that it was because of his advocacy for leading a "prisoner's strike" while he was in jail by going on a fast as a sign of protest to the way they were being treated, especially at mealtime. Prisoners were given their meals without any utensils with which to eat. Because of the protest strike, the situation changed and prisoners were now given food along with utensils, restoring their dignity as human beings and not being treated as animals because they were prisoners.

The truth is that I believed the story was an embell-ishment of the real story and had some doubts about his involvement being as much as he said. I thought that, because of his age, he was unintentionally adding much to an interesting tale. My "teachable moment," however, came when Rumble died. Within a day following his death, I was being contacted by Government personnel and the Governor General's office enquiring about the time and location of the memorial service. Then, the real clincher was the message from the Governor General, Honorable Florizel Glaspole, informing me that he would be attending the service. My first pastoral district, my smallest congregation, apparently one of the least prominent members in the congregation, and now to have the highest government official in the country attending where we will have the service in this very rural community. The answer came to me that Brother Rumble was a community man, a figure of national worth, so his life should be celebrated at the Community Center, which could adequately accommodate a decent crowd. It was during the preparation of his memorial service that his story was confirmed to me, and his history was prepared by others who knew the story. No less than the Governor General himself told about their struggles, which referred to the foundation on which we were building.

I learned then that as a "shepherd," I should never look down on who I may consider the lowest member in my congregation, because that may be the one who could bring to my ministry my greatest moment in the sunlight. It is a lesson that is transferrable to life, a lesson we all can learn for our benefit.

On the day of the funeral service, everything was in place, and I can still see in my mind's eye the green helicopter sheering the trees with the wind from its propellers, landing on the playfield with government officials, including the Governor General alighting and being escorted by security detail and police, and approaching my welcome party before the service began. What an awesome experience for a young preacher! I have since been in the company of many dignitaries, including Prime Ministers and Presidents, but none has ever impacted my ministry as much as this service for humble Brother Rumble.

CALL TO SERVE THE YOUTH

It was while serving here in northern Clarendon that another call came for me to serve the conference in another capacity.

A Conference Session is an event in the Church calendar when officers and departmental directors are considered and elected to serve for a period of three years. This is not always a comfortable time for those who serve because their stewardship could come under scrutiny by the delegates in the session who would decide to return the incumbent or elect someone else. This was my first Conference Session as a worker, and I learned a lot about the internal dynamics of these occasions. When the session was over, a new administration was voted in place under the new leadership of Dr. Cornelius Gray. Dr Gray had recently returned from the United States with a Doctorate in Ministry that attracted some delegates to support him. The feeling among some was that the former administration had served its time, and it was now time for new, younger leadership with new, fresh thinking.

Some who were not reelected were left dejected and dispirited because they thought they were not fairly evaluated and treated. The feeling among some was that the new president had engineered his way by having an inordinate influence on delegates. This set the stage for a very uneasy working relationship and a rather tumultuous time in the history of the Conference. Many vacancies resulted as some workers chose to serve elsewhere. It was not helpful that the new president had not served before in any administrative or departmental office, and his methods and style of leadership were not always appreciated. Many conflicts that arose and were not handled in conventional ways added to the feeling of "us against them," and division among the ranks was the result.

Due to the fact that our youth director, Pastor K. C. Henry, accepted a "service call" to take up a new assignment of pastoral ministry in the Church in London, England, another vacancy emerged.

The church in England was experiencing real cultural, racial, and relational difficulties that needed special attention. One of the solutions that arrived then was to recruit West Indian pastors who could better shepherd the immigrant members, most of whom were from the West Indies and Africa. Pastor Henry was answering that call and consequently left the Youth without an elected leader. I was very shocked when I was tapped by the Conference and told by the Conference Executive secretary that I was voted to serve as acting Youth Director. Because there were still staffing difficulties, I was informed that I would still have to carry my pastoral circuit along with this assignment. As a junior pastor, I was not privileged to negotiate and, in a way, I didn't mind it as I was enjoying my service in the pastorate. I never saw myself as an office person, but since it was going to be an acting position I accepted, but wondered if this was another revelation from God to me that my years as Youth Director, Pathfinder Director, and Federation President were just preparation for this assignment.

What began as an acting position was later confirmed, and I spent seven of the best years of my ministry serving and interacting with the thousands of youth over the Conference territory which, at that time, consisted of five of the fourteen parishes in the country.

I have learned never to say no when God calls, because if He brings you to it, He will bring you through it!

YOUTH MINISTRY YEARS

Serving the youth of the church was the most exciting and satisfying part of my entire ministry. Youth ministry became my passion, and it was not much about what I had to offer, but how, through cooperation and collaboration on any and every task we undertook, we were able to make tremendous successes. There are many youth leaders to thank, and I would not dare to begin naming names because there were so many. The devotion and dedication to the youth by these leaders were very impactful. Each year, those who helped in summer camps as officers would be pressing to get the approved dates for Junior, Teen, and Senior camps that year in order to arrange for time off from work to dedicate this entire time to serving the youth. Today we see many of those youth taking their places in the industry as church workers, engaged in the private and public sectors, also becoming civic leaders, etc, while giving quality, moral, and spiritual leadership, as well as being positive leaders of influence in their respective fields.

OUTSTANDING MEMORIES

One of the things that we looked forward to at camp was the renewal of friendships, how campers had grown and matured, as well as enjoying the many sometimes funny occurrences. One of the other objectives of camp is to help shape and mold the spiritual perspectives of the campers. Sometimes we would run into a camper whose behavior was out of sync with camp norms, and some discipline or sanction had to be applied. If the camper became belligerent, then, as a last resort, such a camper would be sent home. Along with the Camp counselors, we would work diligently with such camper to mitigate the situation and integrate him/her with the other unit members and campers. One of the things we had to be very vigilant about was to ensure that we gave no opportunity to do youthful pranks on their roommates, such as polishing them in their sleep, putting toothpaste on their faces, etc. I have memories of a few situations that we had to handle in order to preserve the ethos of camp. I have selected only two, as well as one that I consider funny to share with you.

I recall this particular camper who came to teen camp and was apparently enjoying camp but thought he could get away with the prank he had dreamed up. At this campsite, there were frogs that would come out, especially at night. This particular day, I was told that he had teased and thrown a frog at a female camper who was mortally afraid of frogs. We called him to our Counsellor's meeting and outlined to him the seriousness of the situation, which could result in his expulsion from camp. He decided that, instead of going home, he would accept as a form of sanction to bring a dozen frogs to line-call the following morning. This was a hard task for him, because he could not start until after suppertime, and he should meet his quota by morning. At line-call he was present with his bag of frogs, so after outlining his infraction to the entire camp, he was called to count them before everyone. Although he met his quota, I was sorry for the frogs, they had been terribly brutalized. I later understood he enlisted some of his roommates to help, as he too was afraid of frogs! This incident earned him the moniker "Froggy" for the rest of his life!

There was this male camper that we were meeting for the first time. He came to Senior camp and was placed in a unit that quickly shunned him because of his obnoxious behavior and for not being a team player. In the units, it was of vital importance that members operate as a team to earn the maximum points possible and earn the highest pennant the next day to post in front of their units. He was a general disruptor, and when his behavior was brought up to camp leadership by the unit Counsellor, we interviewed others from his church and the feedback was not complimentary. So, there was only one decision to make, and that was, "He's going home." When he was called to a meeting of the camp directorate to be interviewed, we finally outlined his infraction and his totally unacceptable behavior, and we decided that he had to go! It was then that we got a real shock with his response. He told us how he had been living with "rejection" all his life, he tried to fit in at church and they rejected him, and now he had come to the only place where he had hoped to find acceptance, and here too he was being rejected. We all began to feel sympathy for him and quickly realized we had to take a totally different course. We listened to his plea as he outlined his home situation, and we decided to temporarily dismiss him and restudied our course of action. We considered that one objective of the camp was to save our youth, and sending him home was counterproductive. We decided the camp Chaplain would be asked to give him special attention, and one of our counselors, who was from his church, would mentor him. When we called him back and outlined the conditions under which he would be allowed to remain, he gratefully accepted and promised to play a different role at camp.

We prayed with him as we ourselves were touched by the moment. To this day, I have not witnessed a more dramatic turnaround in a life that we believed was destined for destruction. We felt that rejection and depression could lead to ultimate suicide without intervention. By the next day, we began to see positive change. He was asked to participate in the devotion, and by the time we had come to the Friday evening, this camper requested baptism in front of all his fellow campers. The greatest miracle of all was his being the speaker for one of the devotions, where he gave his testimony, told his story, and thanked God for camp. I still meet him in congregations in the United States, still faithful to his promise to God. At that devotion, there was hardly a dry eye to be found, including mine.

The third outstanding memory was on the funny

side. One of the things any good camp director would know is that, if the camp was going to be considered a success, the food had to be equal to or better than at home for the youngsters. We usually try to create a good menu that we believe would stimulate the palates of the youth. One day, we thought of changing one of the dinners for a new recipe I had tasted. So, I called Brother Victor Hutchinson, our Camp Food Service Director, and asked him if he had ever tasted the recipe I verbally shared. He said he had never heard of it but was willing to give it a try. So, we decided not to tell anyone ahead of time but would do it the next day. The following day, after line-call, the units were dismissed for dinner, and I took my position in the auditorium to observe the reaction. I was tickled beyond measure when the campers were served and everyone was enquiring what it was. It wasn't rice, it wasn't pumpkin, it wasn't cornmeal, so what was it? No one knew what to call it, but what was obvious was that they were enjoying it immensely. At the end of dinner, there wasn't any left, not even to share with the dogs. The funny part was that, when it came the time for the evening social event, the creative mind among them, led by my deputy director, Ken Wright, had a song ready to be taught and sung about this strange menu they called *Rice-me-pome-to,* signifying what they were able to identify on their plates. Rice, cornmeal, pumpkin, tomato, etc, all rolled into one. I still find that whole event a funny experiment.

PATHFINDERS

Our Pathfinder Clubs were exceptionally active, which gave rise to large investiture services at the sometimes-quarterly parish federation events. There were Federation camps in addition to the regular Conference summer camps, which was one method of developing local leadership. There were Parish Federation Exhibitions when Club members would display craft items they made in club meetings, and after the judging of displays, items would be offered for sale to the thousands who would gather. There were also street marches led by the Spring Village Drum Corps, a local church drum corps, promoting healthy living or any other relevant youth issue at the time. One of the memorable ones was the Rally & March of thousands of Youth, Pathfinders, and Master Guides who gathered at various points of Spanish Town on this Saturday afternoon. At the designated time, the march would begin ahead of police escorts and proceed to the Prison Oval, where all groups marching from various points would converge. This "Oval" was an open space adjoining the St Catherine district prison where hundreds of prisoners do their time of confinement. One of the great benefits of this location was that we were able to address all the prisoners with a message of hope, which would not be possible for us to do otherwise. It was obvious they were grateful as we never forgot the waves, handkerchiefs, rags, or whatever they could find to wave back at us in appreciation. At this location, the program would include addresses from the Government Minister of

Youth, and other public and church officials who addressed the youth and the nation in general. That night, we made the national nightly newscast on Television and radio in a big way. One could feel among the youth the energy, the excitement, the spirit of collaboration and purpose, and the salutation and commendations of the elders that lasted well beyond the event.

It was from this position as Conference Youth Director that I was launched into the arena of Church Administrator when, in a subsequent Conference Session, I was elected to serve as President of the Central Jamaica Conference of Seventh-Day Adventists, which had a membership then of over 40,000 in almost 200 churches and companies. I was succeeded by Pastor Everett Brown, who served with me on many occasions as Camp Chaplain. Today, at the time of writing, he serves as President of the entire Jamaica Union territory.

Pr. Wellington, Youth Director, pinning one pathfinder. Photos by Oswald Wallen, submitted by Pr. Nigel Lewis

(L-R seated) Sister Shirley McPherson, Elder Clifford Cousins, Pastor Nigel Lewis, Pr. Ivor Harry. (Standing in the back) Pr. Noel Allen, Church Pastor (in suit), Pr. Leon Wellington, left of Pr. Allen.

Pathfinders preparing for inspection.

Pathfinders being inspected by Pr. L Wellington escorted by Pr. Nigel Lewis, (then Club Director). In rear, Dr Herbert Golding and Pr. Noel Allen.

Photos by Oswald Wallen, submitted by Pr. Nigel Lewis.

Youth leadership was not without its challenges. It should not be assumed that it was all smooth sailing and wonderfully glorious platitudes. It was some of those challenges to my leadership that helped me to develop my leadership skills, manage conflicts and difficult situations, and also deal with difficult individuals.

One of the coping skills I would develop is not to take these challenges personally, but instead view them as opportunities for personal development. I would retreat to my office or home and prayerfully develop strategies to surmount these difficulties.

I believe it was my mostly successful handling of

these challenges that delegates observed and caused them to think of me as a leader when they were ready to change the Conference leadership at the time.

LAST YOUTH CAMP

The work environment in the Conference had by now become toxic for reasons I will detail later, and what I had not given thought to before was now occupying my mind. Many workers, especially ministerial workers, were migrating quite frequently for work in other conferences and overseas. Some were leaving for educational reasons, so there were many vacancies. Usually, I would spend my vacation time visiting my mother in Toronto, where she lived and where I had many friends. On my last visit, one of my friends enquired again whether I would come to work at the Conference in Canada. Since he was always asking, I said for the first time that if the Conference would extend a "call", I would consider it favorably. So, he went to work, and it was during Camp time in August of 1989, that the acting Conference Secretary, Pastor Fitz Mighty, came to Camp Verley and told me that the President of the Ontario Conference, Pastor Orville Parchment, had called the office to speak with me. He arranged with President Parchment for me to speak with him the following day. As arranged, I left camp in the capable hands of my Deputy Camp director Ken Wright, and was present at the office for the arranged call. As I suspected, it was a job offer at the Ontario Conference and an interview session as well. I was offered a choice of two Churches which were open at the time. I was asked how soon I could take up the appointment, but I had to delay that decision. The Central Conference session was coming up in September, and since I was an elected director, I preferred to present my report, express my gratitude to the delegates, and bid goodbye in a more professional way than to abruptly leave. So, I requested President Parchment a delay of two months, to which he agreed. This would also give me time to tidy up my local business affairs before migrating to Canada.

It was never my intention to discuss my decision to migrate with anyone at the office at that time, but since I did not get the first call from Canada, it was going to be difficult to contain the fact that I was in discussion with the Ontario Conference President. By this time, I was not considered a friend of the conference administration, so any news like that would be welcome, I thought.

Having made my decision to leave, I was now compelled to share with my faithful Camp directors that this Camp meeting would be my last as Director. The next day, I shared with my deputy, Ken Wright, that following the Conference Session I would be taking up a new assignment in Canada. It was really gratifying that, at the end of the Camp, the staff held a most gratifying appreciation session for me, which I have not forgotten and never will as long as life lasts. There were enough staff members to lift me shoulder-high and parade around the auditorium. That's why I love working with young people, they know how to be unpretentious in showing love or disdain!

I soon discovered that word was going around that

Wellington was leaving the Conference, and within a few days, while still at the Camp, some of the prominent workers came to say they heard I was leaving. They were uncomfortable with that because the Conference could no longer continue with the present leadership, and they would want me to become their president. That would be a big decision because I had already given my word to the Administration of the Ontario Conference in Canada. So, I declined the suggestion, because I knew these workers would be in a perilous situation with the administration should their effort fail. A few days after the Camp meeting, I was visited by church elders with much the same plea, and I realized they were not speaking just for themselves. The sentiments for change were very strong. The pressure was indeed building, so I asked for a week to process everything that was going on and how effective I could be in restoring some semblance of unity and fellowship if I were to accept. It would also give me time to talk things over with my wife, and what either decision would mean for the family.

I knew my wife was not keen on moving to Canada because she just can't handle cold weather. Even the parish of Manchester was more than enough for her. So, I sort of suspected what her decision would be. When we discussed the matter, and after praying about it, we finally decided that, since we were already here, if the brethren wanted me to serve them, then I should not disappoint them.

After the expiration of the agreed time, the elders were back to hear the verdict. I finally told them,

"Brethren, you know I have a "call" to serve in Canada, and I have given my word; however, if my Conference wants me to serve, since I'm here already, I will consider your request to stay and serve. But there's one other thing you need to know, and it is that I will not be canvassing any votes for the position." They told me they understood, and I kept my word.

ADMINISTRATIVE RESPONSIBILITIES IN CENTRAL JAMAICA CONFERENCE: DAYS OF CONFLICT

At this point in its history, the Conference was experiencing a period of severe leadership conflict that fractured many relationships among workers, which also affected unity in and among churches. Because many of the relatives of chief players in this conflict are still alive and active, some names will be omitted. But, to remain true to the facts as I know them, some incidences will have to be related to help clarify for some who might not have understood some developments as much as those of us who were close to the action.

Let's take a step back in time and review some developments that brought us to this time of conflict and uncertainties. When our Conference President, Dr. Cornelius Gray, returned to the Conference from his study leave in the United States, I was one of the young workers who viewed him as a good potential leader in our field. I enjoyed an excellent relationship with the then Conference leadership, who hired me a few years earlier. As a matter of fact, I was still an "Intern Pastor," but as a senior person at the time I was given district responsibilities by the Conference, for which I was grateful, and counted with a young family that helped me to be more settled. I was assigned to the Chapelton circuit of Churches in northern Clarendon, with eleven congregations to oversee. My stay in the May Pen circuit was very brief, as I was holding the circuit with the supervision of a senior pastor until their permanent Pastor was appointed. The Conference Committee appointed Dr. Cornelius Gray to take over the Circuit, and I subsequently took up my assignment in Chapelton.

THE CHAPELTON CIRCUIT

This circuit was my first assignment as district Pastor. It was a circuit of eight congregations, mostly small, rural congregations that covered all the upper regions of the parish of Clarendon. I was excited and eager to practice what I had learned about ministry. The Churches welcomed me with open arms, and I enjoyed a fruitful ministry, as well as developed long-lasting friendships.

It was not an easy circuit to manage from many angles. The terrain was difficult, roads were not well maintained all the while, and evangelizing the communities was a challenge. It was a challenge because it was not easy for them to accept "Sabbath Worship" as it would mean such a drastic change to their lifestyle as traditional rural folks.

MY FIRST TENT EVANGELISTIC CAMPAIGN

One outstanding experience I will not forget was my first evangelistic campaign in a new territory called Victoria. The members of the Blackwoods congregation had convinced me that they were making regular visits giving Bible Study to some families in the Victoria community of the parish, who showed great interest in learning more. Youth and idealism got the better part of my judgment, so not enough preparation was done to ensure success. So, we made plans with the Conference to obtain a tent and equipment to impact the community.

This effort being my first tent campaign, I had to wait until after the tent was used by experienced evangelists during the summer months. Our campaign was to be launched in September which happened to be the start of the rainy season. We found a spot on which to pitch the tent, and the day came for us to raise the tent. We were having difficulties getting any help from the community, and then we realized that the community was very much against our presence there.

On one of my visits before the meetings began, I saw a group of about 6-8 young men in a vigorous discussion. Without knowing the topic, I sought to join them. I discovered they were having an animated discussion on current issues. Soon, David, the presumed leader of the group, switched topics and sought to engage me in a discussion on European history. I was astonished at his knowledge of the history, that I only learned as a college student. This engagement really sparked a type of bond that enabled me to extend an invitation to them for the upcoming meetings. It was only sometime later I learned that they were in discussion about how they could obstruct the meetings, as they were gravely opposed to our presence. The sentiments were that they had one church in the small community, and they needed no more.

We were able to commence the meetings with a lot of fanfare but not much community attendance under the tent, no matter if the road in front of the tent was crowded. We decided to keep going, hoping they would gradually drift in.

One thing we did not pay enough attention to was the weather. Victoria is on one of the highest plateaus in the Clarendon Hills, and doing a campaign during late September/early October was not a good idea. Soon, the weather turned out to be quite inhospitable. It was the coldest weather I ever experienced in Jamaica. We could not raise most of the flaps of the tent just to try to keep some warmth under the tent. This didn't help those who were crowding the streets as they were not able to see much, so soon, the numbers became lower and lower. David and some of the group members maintained their interest and would still attend. The rain began to fall on a nightly basis, which would affect our tent, which was perched on a little grade where the soil was soft, and parts of the tent would collapse at times.

It did not take long for us to realize that things were not going well. There were no trees to shelter our tent in this open field as the rains began to pour. Several nights after the meetings and after the rains, the fog came down so thick I had to have people walk on both sides of the road ahead of the car with flashlights in order to navigate safely out of the community. When it rained, my support group, as well as the community, would not show up much for the meetings. Then, the worst thing happened: so much rain fell one day that it took our tent down. This was really deflating, especially in a community that seemed not to welcome us.

We quickly decided to pivot, find a new location, and complete our meetings elsewhere. Our new location below the plateau was much more hospitable, both from the community and the weather standpoint. We saw many conversions to Christ and subsequent baptisms. Among those who eventually got baptized was David, the presumptive leader of that group I met in Victoria. Having observed his interest in history and the brilliance he displayed, I knew all he needed was the right opportunity to become an asset to society. I quickly arranged for him to be registered at the then-West Indies College, where he could work and study at the same time. Today, David is considered a part of our family and a successful entrepreneur in the local tourist industry, owning and managing his own business in the Montego Bay area. This evangelistic experience ended on a successful note, and I learned many life lessons from that exposure!

LOCAL MINISTERIAL FRATERNITY ET AL.

While I lived in Chapelton, I was able to work well with Pastors of other denominations, as we formed a local Ministerial Fraternity, and would rotate in each other's homes for fellowship and prayer, and to discuss solutions to community issues monthly.

In the parish of Clarendon, there were now three of us as Adventist pastors namely, Pastor Joseph Hutchinson, Pastor Gladstone Knight, my batchmate, and myself. Before Dr Gray's arrival in the parish, Pastor Hutchinson was the Ordained pastor in the parish who was assigned by the Conference to assist us as Junior Pastors with baptisms and weddings. That helped us develop a bond as we were roughly in the same age grouping. When Dr. Gray arrived in the parish, he became the senior pastor, and naturally, a fraternal alliance developed, as we all thought we could learn much from his experience, his practice of ministry over the years, and especially I that was the pastoral presence in the circuit before his arrival.

The political situation in the country was very tumultuous as then Prime Minister Michael Manley and his government was experimenting with "Democratic Socialism," and the opposition, Jamaica Labour Party, was very much opposed and was espousing the virtues of "Capitalism". Many people were of the view that the United States Government through the CIA was behind the upheavals that were taking place, in order to undermine Manley's administration. There were shortages of food and domestic supplies on a scale we had never experienced before, and many necessary household commodities disappeared from the supermarket shelves. When these commodities became available, the prices usually skyrocketed, but interestingly, after the Manley Administration lost the general elections, food supplies returned to normal within weeks. As Pastors, we would meet at one of our member's grocery shops on Fridays to get our supplies at modest prices and hassle-free. Out of these usual Friday meetings, the idea of a monthly meeting with each pastoral family on a rotating basis was for fellowship, spiritual support, and the discussion of challenges we may have encountered in administering our circuits.

THE CJC MINISTERIAL FRATERNITY

We found so fulfilling these fraternal meetings, that we decided to recommend the idea to others for the formation of a conferencewide ministerial fraternity. The idea eventually was accepted and approved by the Conference administration after a presentation to the Conference Committee by Dr. Orlando Moncrieffe, who outlined the objectives of the fraternity. Following the provisional approval by the committee, a group was established to develop the constitution that would guide the organization, which would then be approved by the committee. Dr Orlando Moncrieffe was asked to lead this group and I was privileged to be one of the members of that commission. The Central Jamaica Conference Ministerial Fraternity was established and I was asked to serve as its first president.

We soon discovered that the Conference administrators were becoming very uncomfortable with the Fraternity and those of us who were serving in the Parish of Clarendon. The feeling was being entertained among them that the organization was established as a platform to overthrow the administration. We were flabbergasted at the thought as our only motive was to develop a more knowledgeable and rounded Pastor, help junior pastors to grow, as well as to develop better ministerial practice not just in one parish, but among pastors throughout the entire conference.

The development of the Ministerial Fraternity was generally welcomed by the pastoral workforce and became an integral part of the ministerial life and practice in the conference until today.

Because Dr. Gray and the conference leaders were more contemporaries, he felt comfortable challenging them on some of the positions they were taking and the things they were saying. The challenge and response became sharper, and we junior ministers found that we were being included in the ideological struggle and treated with suspicion regarding our views about administration! The financial situation of the conference was in bad shape and the auditor's reports were less than complimentary, which caused much angst among the administration, as there were pastors who were ready to challenge the administration. It was obvious that they were becoming gravely concerned at the actions and utterances of some pastors at workers' meetings and elsewhere, and reacted badly. This would not be a comfortable situation for any administration since the conference session was imminent. It was clear that this session would not be business as usual.

THE 3RD TRIENNIAL CONFERENCE SESSION

The Conference Session began in an atmosphere of real tension, alliances were being formed between those who were advocating change and those who wanted to retain the then administration. This being my first session as a worker/employee, while I maintained a keen interest in the proceedings, I was more prepared to observe rather than become too involved. The program proceeded well on the opening night. The real tension came to the fore the following day when reports from the administration and departmental directors were to be presented, as well as the establishment of the various committees essential to the proceedings of the session.

The report that sparked the greatest discussion was the Treasurer's report. As I mentioned earlier, the conference finances were not in good shape as workers were having challenges even with getting their salary on time. The report that was presented gave a much more optimistic picture than the one the workforce was experiencing, which became the trigger point. The discussion was very sharp from the delegate standpoint, and we wondered how things would really end. When the time for reactions expired, the report was voted but there was much disquiet. The Nominating Committee was finally selected and went to work. The delegation anxiously awaited the results from the committee. From the trend of the discussion and the sentiments generated by the discussion, it was generally felt that it would not be a favorable result for the administration.

After a lengthy wait, during which other reports

were presented by the departmental directors, the Union President, who by the constitution chairs the committee, and the secretary of the committee emerged and ascended the platform to give the report. The air was thick with anticipation and suspense. After the usual preliminaries, the Secretary proposed the name of Dr. Cornelius Gray as president of the conference. All kinds of emotions were on display, but when the vote was taken, Dr. Gray was voted to serve as president, Pastor James Westley as Secretary, and Pastor Henry Mitchell as treasurer.

This was the beginning of a new, but turbulent era for the conference. It was a perfect setup for conflicts between persons with large egos and different perspectives on the future. Many new Directors were elected with only a few being retained from the previous administration. The sentiments between these polarized groups were less than charitable, as the new administration handled many issues from the standpoint of victors versus the vanquished. And the unfortunate thing was that these sentiments overflowed into various congregations which shared much of the sentiments of the pastors who shepherded them. There were many members who were unhappy and discouraged by the situation, but they remained loyal to their faith in Christ and continued to serve and pray earnestly.

THE NEW ADMINISTRATION

My assessment of the situation as it occurred then was that Dr. Gray meant well, and had some good leadership skills, but poor human relationship skills which brought him into many unnecessary conflicts. He wanted to see the conference grow in every way, and in many ways it did. He was an aspirational leader and tried to inspire the workforce to set and achieve large evangelistic goals and under his leadership, the financial situation of the conference improved significantly over time. It was a time of explosive evangelistic growth through the holding of many tent evangelistic campaigns. He believed in the involvement and training of the laity. It was through his great emphasis on the laity that the great international evangelist, Fitz Henry and several others, blossomed and bloomed. Although Evangelist Henry was from the East Jamaica Conference, when it was brought to Dr. Gray's attention that Henry wanted to launch out in big tent evangelism, he embraced the opportunity to offer him a tent to evangelize one of the new Portmore communities. Henry was having difficulty with leadership in the East as, apparently, he did not have the confidence in himself to successfully effect such a large evangelistic outreach. He didn't have the formal preparation and, further, this would be his first major effort, and tent meetings were very costly. It was reported that Henry had already pitched a tent at "S Corner," one of the most volatile areas in the city of Kingston, but was not allowed to proceed by the administration. This brought on some discouragement, but Henry was still burning with passion to preach the word.

The appropriate contacts were made, and Dr. Gray Invited Evangelist Henry to come over and do an evangelistic campaign in the new community of Waterford, in St. Catherine, and gave him the full backing of the Conference with financing and bible workers along with the strong pastoral support of Pastor Joseph Hutchinson. This became one of the most spectacular events at the time. The preacher brought such creativity to bear upon his powerful exposition of the scriptures, that it became a real sensation. The crowds were spectacular, the excitement was palpable, music was rich and lively. At the end of the campaign, 276 new members were baptized, which resulted in the organization of the Waterford Seventh-day Adventist Church two years later with a membership of 556. Pastor Hutchinson reminded me that at that time, Waterford was the only Church in the Inter-American Division to have such a large membership for its inauguration into the "Sisterhood of Churches." The Portmore Church, worshipping in less than ideal conditions in a rented building, could not accommodate this large influx of members, so, with no other building to send the new believers, the tent became their church until land was found nearby the tent site and was purchased for the new congregation. This church continues to be one of the largest and most progressive congregations in the Central Conference. This also marked the beginning of a long and productive relationship with the evangelists and an evangelistic career that took Evangelist Henry to the United Kingdom, the Caribbean islands, and as far away as Malawi and Johannesburg, South Africa, where he conducted the first and largest satellite campaign sponsored by the General Conference and covered several countries on the continent of Africa. It was reported that at the end of the satellite campaign, over 20,000 people became members of the church.

This evangelistic momentum that Dr. Gray generated by engaging Evangelist Fitz Henry attracted other lay evangelists such as now Pastor Franklyn Jackson, Austin Hines, Brother Lascelles Davis, and later Errol Long from the East Conference. Their work along with our local lay preachers and the pastoral efforts, helped to make the Central Conference the leading Conference in the Union for many consecutive years in soul-winning endeavors.

THE MAY PEN HIGH SCHOOL

One of the casualties that resulted from the change of administration, and what I see as a conflict between two men with large egos, was the loss to the denomination of the May Pen High School. This School was one of the first schools in the conference and started then by the initiative of Pastor Harold Bennett and the members of the May Pen Church. This School had been a well-respected high school for years producing many graduates who later moved on to become workers of the church and many other professions.

Mr. Winston Preddie was appointed principal by the former administration, to succeed, then Principal, Mrs. Esther Coleman. Preddie was one of our exceptional principals who threw himself fully into whatever he was doing, and teaching was his passion, so he did very well. Youth ministry and youth involvement were his life. He served for many years as deputy camp director, conducted evangelistic campaigns, and was beloved by many. But he was also a strong-willed and determined individual who was disappointed by the results of the Conference Session and was strongly resentful of the new President, and I would classify the feeling of the President as mutually resentful. Without delving into more detail, the situation only grew worse as the years went by, making May Pen one of the epicenters of discontent and fermentation of negative feelings towards the administration. The result was that after the administration failed to remove Mr. Preddie from being the principal, the Conference Committee voted to close the High School, transferring some and dismissing the rest of the workers. Following this dramatic action at the Conference, Mr. Preddie decided to keep the institution open with all the workers who were not transferred. While I admit that the relationship between the management of the High School and the conference has improved tremendously over time, the situation continues unresolved until the time of writing.

I was now serving as Secretary of the Central Conference with Dr. Gray as President. In the midst of all this turmoil, discontent, and resentment, I was asked to serve as interim pastor of the same May Pen circuit until a permanent replacement was found. I would be pastoring a divided congregation in which many of the prominent leaders decided to withdraw their support and involvement. These were members and leaders I had worked with on my previous posting in that circuit; they knew me and I knew them. I enjoyed a good relationship then, but this time was different. I was determined, however, that I would give my best to serve as impartially as I could, with those who were willing. Being Secretary of the Conference was not helpful to the relationship with those who were anti-administration. Any decision of the Conference that had to be communicated would go out over my signature, so I was viewed by those people as part of the problem.

I could never say I was ever disrespected while I served, except on one occasion when I was attending a board meeting at the church, and at the end, when I was ready to leave, I discovered that two of my car tires had been deliberately deflated! I could not say the same, however, for the new incoming Pastor, who after I had introduced him to the congregation was physically assaulted by one member. I was greatly disturbed, and as my last act at the church, through the Church Board, we got the perpetrator to submit a written apology by a specified time and recommended a further sanction of three months for the act, which brought the church into public disrepute. The Pastor was installed and had a very fruitful ministry in the circuit.

As Conference secretary, I saw one of my roles as playing a positive role in helping to heal wounds and be a buffer between the administration and those feeling aggrieved for one reason or another. In administrative meetings, I would give what I considered to be helpful advice and suggestions as to how things could be handled better and more diplomatically.

I soon discovered that my advice and suggestions were not really appreciated, but rather construed as my usurping presidential authority and trying to run the administration. I was determined to maintain my independence, which admittedly was difficult while remaining part of the administration. Little by little, I realized I was being distanced from some discussions and so I began to react by doing that which fell under my portfolio but would avoid some of the casual fellowship sessions.

I realized that I would be serving for only one session as Secretary, therefore when the next session arrived, I was not surprised that I was succeeded by Pastor Joseph Hutchinson as Secretary. No one knew, except close friends, how glad I was to be relieved of the position because that gave me back my independence. I pretended to be unhappy by staying away from chit-chat sessions after the morning devotions. I did not volunteer ideas or responses on the committee, even about portfolios I previously held unless specifically asked, then I would freely share. All this was my deliberate attempt to stay outside the circle of which I had no desire to become part of again.

In the Conference Session, I retained my position as Director of the Youth and the Health Ministries. This was going to be a trying term for me, because I was no longer part of the inner circle, but was still viewed with great suspicion. Programs I developed for the departments within my portfolio were attacked and undermined chiefly by a few pastors and laity friends of the administration, but I found much success and support from the laity and pastors in the field.

By nature, I am not a conflict-oriented person, so the

prevailing scenario made it easy for me to accept that invitation to serve at the Ontario Conference in Canada. What I didn't realize was that many members were observing and were also unhappy with my being left out of some conference activities.

As a case in point, I was attending a Parish Convention in Port Maria at which I was challenged by the Youth Federation President, who was a close friend of the President, regarding a promotion I had made at the Youth department. During the lunch break, I was summoned to a brief meeting by the President, in which I was threatened with being fired for my actions. I quickly retaliated by challenging the statement with, "Try it if you dare!" I could do that because, having been elected by the Constituents in a session and not by appointment of the committee, I could only be fired by the Committee if I had compromised myself, but certainly not for executing my portfolio. After that encounter was over, I was called over by a very senior Elder who was a little distance away but understood the dynamics of what was going on since the session. He said to me, "Pastor, I don't know what the nature of that meeting was, but I see you were under attack, but don't worry, we are praying for you and things will work out in time." I told him I had no idea he was noticing, but yes, I was being attacked for the promotion I had made, which some people were not happy with. I thanked him and asked that they continue their prayers for the situation.

These were some of the uncomfortable situations

that caused much disquiet among the workforce and leadership feeling threatened.

THE 6TH TRIENNIAL CONFERENCE SESSION (SEPTEMBER 12 – 14, 1989)

The Sixth Triennial Session of the conference was approaching, and the administration was doing everything to ensure that they were returned to office. However, many of the workers and leaders who felt exhausted by the prevailing disunity and conflicts were thinking and talking about making changes, but they would give no indication to those who were loyal to the administration of how they would accomplish this change at the session. The administration by then had made itself very unpopular to so many members and denominational workers, that it was almost a foregone conclusion that they were in a self-destruct mode and would not be returned to office. In preparation for the Conference Session, there was the usual call to all churches to engage in prayer and fasting the week before the session was to convene. The focus of prayer was that God would take charge of the session, bring about unity, and focus on the mission rather than the individual's selfish desires. The Church prayed, and I just imagined the conflicting prayers God was listening to, but remained confident that God was and still is in charge of His Church and will do the right thing that fulfill His purposes.

It was during this unsettled time that after hearing that I was on my way out, some elders and church workers visited to have a talk with me. Their concern was that they could no longer support the then administration based upon the prevailing disquiet, and there was a strong desire to have me serve as President for the next term. This was a big problem because I had already given my word to the Ontario Conference President, said goodbye to my youth leaders, and my last act was to read my triennial report, thank the constituency for the privilege to serve them, and develop my ministry among them. My mind was already in a transitional mode, but now here comes this request. These were influential leaders who came, and they were very sincere in their desire to have me serve. We agreed that I could not give an answer then, as I would have to make this a matter of prayer, and also have a talk with my wife about this very life-changing matter. We agreed on a time the following week to give a response. I believe they were praying as I was that God would guide us in making the right decision, for truly it was not an easy one for us. My wife and I talked and prayed for God to help us in this decision, and her response was that we are here already, and if the brethren wanted me to serve them, I should not deny them, and looking back I believe God did show His hand.

At the time appointed, they returned to get my response. I was able to say to them that they were fully aware that I had a "call" to Canada, which was very attractive since my mother was living permanently there and alone. If they believed that my serving would help restore the peace and unity to the conference, then if I'm asked, I would accept, but with one caveat that I would not be canvassing anyone for support, and they knew I would keep my word.

This consultation happened just days before we were scheduled to gather at Camp Verley for the big convocation. Our special guest at this session was the President of the Inter-American Division, Dr. George Brown. He was not unaware of the tension and difficulties through which the conference was going through, as many members and workers had written letters of appeal to him for help in the situation. It was a large expectant crowd that came to the opening exercises of the session, which was not unusual for Central Conference. Brother George Planto was chosen to lead the song service and among his choice of songs was "Master the Tempest is Raging," and indeed it was a spiritual tempest. The Conference President rendered his report, which was well received because it showed there was growth in many vital areas of the work. Since it was now late in the night, following the seating of delegates, the accepting new congregations into the sisterhood of churches, and an inspiring message from President George Brown, no further business was attempted and the program ended for the night.

The real action was to begin with the next day's business session, where the nominating committee would be selected. The selection process ran into some difficulties when it was discovered that there was a duplication of delegates from some churches. What really happened was that when the President discovered that some delegates were not in support of his re-election, he used an executive committee to change some delegates with substitutes from names submitted by his supportive pastors. The problem, though, was that the original delegates voted by the Conference committee came with their letters of credentials, but were unable to register as others had registered in their places. At this point, Dr. George Brown was asked for his guidance, and to resolve the situation he asked all those with letters of the most recent date to stand on one side, and those with letters of the earlier date to stand on the other side. Then he asked those with letters of recent date to remove their delegate badges and pass them over to the originally voted delegate(s) from their churches.

Any casual observer of these processes would have seen clearly that at this point the "die was cast." The process continued, the working (large) Committee was selected and proceeded to select all committees neces-sary for the smooth functioning of the session, including the twenty-one members of the Nominating Committee. The Nominating Committee sat, did its work, and then returned to the auditorium to render its recommenda-tion for the office of President. You could see and almost feel the anticipatory tension in the air as everyone waited with bated breath. When the secretary of the Nominating Committee read the recommendation to put in nomination the name Pastor Leon Wellington, the auditorium erupted with spontaneous and thunderous applause. When the applause subsided, the chairman was able to carry forward the voting process. It was during this process that it became obvious that the incumbents were not about to take the report without objection, so Pastor Peter Kerr moved a motion that the report be returned to the committee. The motion was overwhelmingly defeated, and the recommendation overwhelmingly approved, and one could see and feel the relief on the faces of the great majority of the delegates. So, God and the delegates made the decision for me, and I was on to another trajectory in life.

THE NEXT LEG OF THE JOURNEY: OUR FIRST QUADRENNIUM

On September 14, 1989, the Nominating Committee recommended and the delegation voted the following people as Officers and Directors for various departments for the ensuing triennium.

- President: Leon B. Wellington
- Secretary: Milton G. Gregory
- Treasurer: Wellesley H. Gunter
- Church Ministries:Donald E. Kent
- Sabbath School: Milton G. Gregory
- Lay-Activities: Donald E. Kent
- Youth Ministry: Everette E. Brown
- Stewardship: Noel Allen
- Publishing Director: Henry R. E. Smith
- Health & Temperance: Claude L. Brown
- Communication Director: Patrick L. Allen
- Home & Family Life: Wellesley H. Gunter
- Ministerial Secretary: Leon B. Wellington
- Religious Liberty: Leon B. Wellington
- Trust Services: Noel Allen
- Auditor: Everton Nathan

With the session now ended, the real work for the newly elected administrators was to heal old wounds, unite the broken spirits of some members of the workforce, and prosecute the real mission of the church.

To accomplish this mammoth task, we quickly realized that we needed Divine help. Our first task was to organize a three-day retreat in order to interact, pray for guidance, and plan strategies for a successful triennium with the new departmental leaders and Conference Committee members.

Almost overnight the mood of the conference changed, not so much by what we were able to do, but just by the sense that a new beginning had come, the feeling of a fresh wind blowing through the atmosphere, and a general anticipation of moving forward with a spirit of cooperation, collaboration, and understanding. This by itself posed a challenge to the new administration. Could we deliver what was expected? That's why this retreat was so needed and proved to be a real blessing to the team. We were able to coalesce as a team and around common goals for future action.

Today, I can say that God really came through with and for us, as we saw success in every area of ministry. The finances grew, and evangelism was lighting every corner of the territory, led by pastors and lay persons alike with the reaping of thousands of new believers. The Conference continued to be the leading entity in the evangelism of the then-six fields of the Union. This is not to say that everyone who was opposed to our administration was now converted, but the pervading sentiments were so positive, it was difficult to be negative.

TURKS & CAICOS ISLANDS

One of the things our committee had to address was the need for a pastor to serve in the Turks and Caicos Islands. These Islands were part of the West Indies Union, and each Conference in the Union was responsible on a rotating basis to provide a pastor to serve for the Triennium. It was Central Jamaica's turn to fill the spot, and who would it be? I had never visited the Islands before but only knew enough by what those who had served were willing to share. When we discussed the Issue as an administration, one name kept coming to the fore, Pastor Peter Kerr. As you may recall, it was he who had the courage to stand up at the Conference Session and opposed my election by moving a motion to return the report that brought my name into nomination. It would be very difficult for one not to decide that the administration was getting back at him with a plan to exile him by this assignment. What I knew was that the Pastor was an excellent preacher and organizer, and had leadership skills that he could develop in a territory that needed skills like his. I also knew it would be a better environment for him at the moment, not from the administration's standpoint, but more from his colleagues who saw things differently and did not appreciate the role he played.

The three churches on three different Islands needed real attention from someone who could build its very small membership of over 140. I believe Pastor Kerr would think my motives were not pure, so I decided to ask our Conference Secretary, Pastor Gregory, to speak with him to ascertain how disposed he was to accept this assignment. He was able to convince the pastor that he could make a real difference and we were willing to recommend him as president and give him all the support needed; he accepted the proposal, we processed his name through the Committee, and recommended him to the West Indies Union. We know now that God was leading in this appointment, as Pastor Kerr's ministry prospered greatly, and the Turks and Caicos field experienced exponential growth under his leadership.

When in future years as President of the Union I was able to visit Pastor Kerr, the reality of what he had to deal with was revealed to me. Truly it was not a promising field unless someone was prepared to work hard. The one church on North Caicos had been closed so long a tree had grown up in the middle of the old building, and men with a big saw had to be employed to cut it down. The lone denominational school in middle Caicos had long closed. What was the only church building had been inhabited and eaten out by duck ants, and the few remaining members worshipped in the small chapel of the nearby morgue which had to be shared at times with a corpse or two! Certainly, location-wise was not a good prospect for growth. Only the very brave would accept invitations to night meetings in a morgue, so none could be held!

Pastor Kerr's ministry grew and prospered despite

the challenges he faced and deserves our greatest accolades for his commitment and dedication to duty. He worked hard and served well, and when it was time for him to leave the Islands to serve as secretary of the new Atlantic Caribbean Union, which was organized out of the West Indies Union, the membership in the Islands had grown to over 3000, one secondary school, and 6 congregations. Today, Pastor Kerr serves as President of the Atlantic Caribbean Union with headquarters located in Nassau, Bahamas, and the organizational status of Turks and Caicos Islands is now upgraded to a conference. Indeed, what hath God wrought!

Back in Central Jamaica, we learned in a practical way that church leadership is not the same as corporate leadership with a CEO who hands down directives. We learned and remained conscious that developing good public relationships, as well as good personal relationships, go a long way in leading members who in general are "volunteers" and respond differently from the way CEOs relate to employees. The model of spiritual leadership that generally succeeds is that which presents and can be best viewed as "Servant leadership." It was our determination to avoid anything that would perpetuate or lead us down the path taken by the previous administration, which brought so much division and hurt feelings.

The triennium was now coming to an end, and we soon learned that those Pastors who had not fully accepted the results of the last session were planning to invite one of our former workers, Dr. Patrick Allen, who left the workforce earlier on leave to study for his doctorate at Andrews University, to return to take over the leadership of the conference. I knew almost every meeting they were having because they were so bent on recruiting support, that their method was quite untidy. Obviously, not everyone appreciated their *modus operandi,* so we were kept abreast of activities. For instance, one evening, on my way back to Spanish Town, I was able to pass by the meeting place and observe all who were in attendance. I did not attend or disturb, for that was unnecessary as I was updated on the agenda at the close of the meeting. We were having no meetings because, as I did not canvass anyone at the beginning, I was not about to change that now.

We had our last workers' event at Hellshire Beach, at which I addressed the group. I gave them notice that whereas I was fully aware of the activities of some, I would say nothing to them until after the session. The inappropriate electioneering method they employed, which we hoped had died with the last administration, was sadly still alive and well. By then, I knew that their group would be of minor influence at the session and that we had a good chance of re-election. We knew their chosen candidate would be coming to Jamaica at the time of the session, but he never attended the event. This is an issue he and I spoke about sometime later.

The quadrennial ended on a very triumphant note based on the reports presented to the delegates, in which we recounted the many blessings God had poured upon us during the term.

SOME NOTABLE ACHIEVEMENTS

Parish Action Committees

One of the things we were able to establish in the Conference was what we named the Parish Action Committees. These committees were constituted by the Pastors in the Parish and lay leaders from the Churches representing each pastoral circuit. This idea at the time was a revolutionary one. The reason that inspired their creation was the fact that at every meeting of the Conference Committee, there would be so many requests for grants to help churches with differing needs such as roofing, land acquisitions, those getting ready for dedication, and church construction. On almost every occasion, the requests would far outstrip our ability to supply according to available allocated resources. In addition, with the five parishes of Clarendon, Manchester, St. Ann, St. Mary, and St. Catherine, with churches large and small to attend, there was always the issue of equity. The committee of laypersons from the churches in each parish with their pastors would review each request, and allocate the neediest cases available to the Parish as a recommendation to the Conference committee. The Conference Committee would review the recommendations and if all falls within budget, vote and forward the cheques to respective congregations. The funding of the PACs was done by the Treasury Department on a quarterly basis, and in addition, the overflow from the annual Harvest Ingathering campaign goals for each Parish was allocated as an additional source of funding for the Parish Committees.

Leaving the overflow from each parish within that parish provided a great motivation not only for the Ingathering campaign but also to go beyond to benefit the churches. It is one of those innovations that continues to benefit the churches today.

Parish Conventions

While the annual parish conventions were not an innovation for us, it was the re-programming that made the difference. Conventions by then had become just routine and boring, with reduced attendance each year. People would come for the fellowship, the preaching, and the music, but the continuous promotion by the departments that would take up the rest of the day would see many leaving early, and few of the younger people attending because they didn't find most of the promotion relevant to their interests. We studied the situation and then decided to use the morning section of the program for spiritual instructions, motivation, and promotions. The afternoon would involve promotions from the educational and health institutions, then breakout groups for all other departments simultaneously for an hour, more time than would be available in a general gathering. Those attendees who were not attending as departmental personnel would be in a special session on a selected theme. The response to this new programming was overwhelming. Capacity was the challenge for many subsequent conventions, as departmental directors and their personnel had more time for interaction, learning, and promotion.

Our Second Quadrennium

The administration was returned for another four years by an overwhelming vote of confidence by the delegates. The second term continued with the momentum we enjoyed during the first term. I believe we had two of the most successful terms as we were able to turn the tide of negative sentiments and feelings, develop greater cohesion among the workforce and membership, as well as meet the financial and soul-winning objectives we had set for the Conference.

During the session, which was held at the usual Camp Verley venue, the Central Jamaica Campsite, the energy was very upbeat and spiritually warm. The reports were presented and approved by the delegates, which resulted in the re-election of the team with minor adjustments at the departmental level.

After we had our planning retreat and orientation of new departmental leadership, we returned to regular work at the office, and it was time to keep my promise to those who waged that negative campaign against the administration. So, I made individual appointments to meet with the principal leaders of the group that opposed the return of my administration. These interviews, some thought, even the individuals themselves, would be recriminatory. The principal purpose of those meetings was to be likened to a counseling session regarding the expectation of church members as well as the organization and the community regarding proper protocol and appropriate behavior by gospel workers, especially pastors. I remember saying to each of them that you may not have the opportunity to organize against me again, but what I want you to know and accept is that your method was wrong, and you should never again use that method to select leadership for this church when there is an established method that will always yield the results the Church and the Lord desires. While it was uncomfortable for some of them, I felt I had done my duty as a leader. The meeting was very amicable, and several expressed their appreciation for the manner in which this session was conducted. One, I recall, was helped with tissue to dry the tears. We prayed together and that became a turning point for those in question. It was only years later, in another place and another time, that I understood how impactful the meeting was when one of the persons involved called and spent more than an hour on the phone with me, expressing his gratitude for the leadership I gave, the counseling sessions we had, and how it all helped to shape his ministry. Today, he continues to serve the Church as a very loved, successful Pastor in the United States.

Third Term Quadrennium

The third term was approaching, and we engaged in the usual preparation for another successful session program. We had good news to share with the delegates of God's abundant blessings. The Conference had reached a level of operational efficiency and transparency with which the delegates were obviously satisfied, so when the session concluded, we were again re-elected for a third term. The delegates, however, made an adjustment to the team, by electing a new secretary in the person of pastor Donald Kent. Many of those who would be delegates at the upcoming union session, decided that they would make a change because if the opportunity presented itself, as they fully expected some retirements, they would be recommending my name to serve in the West Indies Union office. Should that happen, then it would be an easy transition to a new president in the person of Pastor Kent.

I was by this time the senior president among the six, which stood me in good stead if asked, to serve the West Indies Union in an administration or departmental position. In any case, I did not see myself standing for another term as President of the Central Conference, so it would soon be time to move on to another challenge anyway. That was the reason I mentioned in the counseling session with those pastors that they may not have the opportunity to organize against me again because I had determined not to stand for Conference President after that term ended. As is my custom, I would thrust my future in God's hands, because I believed with all my heart that He would do what is best for me. As I indicated earlier, to be a minister was not my choice, so in all things, I was prepared to let the Lord take the lead. We organized our usual retreat following the conference session and then set off to work for another term. The West Indies Union Session would be only two months away, so one of the first responsibilities to which our committee addressed itself was the selection of the delegates to represent our conference in that session.

4
WEST INDIES UNION CONFERENCE

SEVENTH-DAY ADVENTIST CHURCH
ADMINISTRATIVE STRUCTURE

What is the West Indies Union Conference? A "Union" is the next higher level of the Seventh-day Adventist Church structure from the Conference. A Union is comprised of a number of Conferences within a contiguous region that have been grouped for administrative effectiveness under the supervision of the Union. The "Union" is governed by its constitution, which allows it to operate tertiary institutions such as Hospitals, Colleges, and Universities.

A "Conference" is comprised of a number of churches within a designated geographic area, with its own administrative responsibilities and governed by its own constitution. Conferences are permitted by its constitution to operate primary and secondary institutions such as Primary, High Schools, and Clinics. The

West Indies Union, as structured then, was comprised of the countries of the Bahamas, Cayman Islands, Turks and Caicos Islands, and Jamaica. and the Administrative headquarters were located in Mandeville.

Conferences usually operate on a four-year cycle when a session is scheduled to receive reports from its elected officers of their stewardship for that period and answer how they have addressed the voted action plans at the previous session. Each organized church is entitled to select delegates according to its membership, to represent them by receiving the reports, receive newly organized congregations into the "sisterhood of churches," and voting new leadership for the ensuing four years.

Unions usually convene their sessions on a five-year cycle and draw their delegates from the Conferences and institutions they operate. For every level of church structure, the laity is well represented and participates in all aspects, including the question-and-answer sessions following the reports presented by elected officials. This can be very vigorous as professionals and others probe deeper for answers. It is at these sessions that the Church is put back into the hands of the members when they have full authority to determine what action plans they need the administration to attend in the ensuing session.

The next level above the "Union" is the General Conference, which administers the church on a worldwide basis. The General Conference administers the worldwide work through what is known as its "Divisions of the General Conference." These Divisions administer regions of the world field through its constitution, but is not a constituent level, being a division of the General Conference. At this point, the General Conference administers its work around the world through thirteen Divisions. The advantage to the members is that the "Divisions" operate closer to the people in their regions, and are better able to address social, political, and religious issues occurring in the region that may impact the mission of the church. Division leaders are elected at the expiration of the five-year term when the world conference convenes its session at the designated location, voted five years earlier.

MY NEXT MOVE

The time had arrived for the West Indies Union Conference to hold its "Fourth Quinquennial Session" at the Mandeville Church, in Manchester. At that time the officers of the Union were Dr. Silas McKinney, a native of the Bahamas, Pastor Meremoth Weir as Executive Secretary, and Elder Aston Barnes as Treasurer. The message of our Division President, Dr. George Brown, was a powerful inspiration that laid a good foundation for a very spirit-filled session. The reports of its directors and institutions of the Union were very encouraging as they showed that God was blessing the work. The new officers recommended by the Nominating Committee and voted by the delegation to serve for the ensuing five years were, Dr. Silas McKinney as President, Pastor Leon Wellington as Executive Secretary, and Elder Aston Barnes as Treasurer.

A new chapter had begun, and therefore it was time for me to organize with my conference Committee for the selection of a replacement before I could make the transition. In such a situation, it is the Union that supervises the process. At the convening of a special meeting of the Central Jamaica Conference Executive Committee, Pastor Donald Kent was selected to serve the rest of the four-year term. With that, the transition was complete, and I was now free to assume my new position. It was an interesting learning experience at the Union level, and so many things were transpiring at the same time. I was the youngest of the officers, but it was such a real pleasure to work alongside these men of experience with whom I would serve as a team. There was a great spirit of camaraderie, and we developed a real spiritual brotherhood which continued until the passing of Dr. Silas McKinney and continues with Elder Aston Barnes and Dr. Noel Fraser of whom I will speak later. I can say with a great deal of satisfaction that I was privileged to work with men who displayed such Christlike qualities, served unselfishly, loved the church, and were strong apologists for the gospel.

There was a time several years ago when there was a very strong discussion on whether this level of church organization was necessary for the organizational structure of the church. I believe that those who were calling for the abolishment of the Unions were a call from the uninformed. One of the great strengths of the Seventh-day Adventist church is the way it is organized globally for efficiency and effectiveness. While Conferences supervise the day-to-day needs of the local churches, the Union is responsible for supervising the Conferences and local missions, as well as Institutions it may operate such as Colleges/Universities, Hospitals, Book Centers, Food factories, etc. While the conferences record the statistics of each member, only the local congregation may admit/accept an individual into membership or withdraw/deny membership from anyone who unfortunately fails to live up to his or her baptismal commitments. In other words, regardless of the level in the organization in which one functions, such an individual must belong to a local congregation.

LEADERSHIP TRANSITION

Dr. Silas McKinney was one of our revered and visionary leaders who did a lot to enhance the development of the church employees as well as the institutions of the Union namely, West Indies College, now Northern Caribbean University, Andrews Memorial Hospital, Westico Foods, The Capital Development Fund and the Publishing Ministry. Under his leadership, West Indies College as it was known then was given great institutional support during the presidency of Dr. Herbert Thompson, who demonstrated a clear vision of the role the College should play in the nation and beyond by having well-prepared graduates who can then contribute to Church development and growth as well as to nation building.

It was also a time of expansion for the Andrews Memorial Hospital under the steady hand and visionary leadership of Dr. Patrick Rutherford. It is to be noted that these two institutional leaders began their tour of leadership about the same time Dr. McKinney was elected to serve the Union as president. So I think that helped to create a certain kind of dynamism that saw the institutions growing at an unprecedented rate. McKinney was willing to do whatever it took to see these young visionary leaders succeed. This was the time also that the Capital Development Fund established by the Union was in a strong growth mode, which helped the institutions grow by making developmental loans available and much less than regular commercial rates for their structural and equipment needs.

Almost simultaneous with my arrival at the Union office in 1995, the Committee voted to remodel the office building. I was asked to supervise that construction with Mr. Jeffrey Wiles as our assigned builder. So, the present structure was upgraded and rededicated.

After two years in his third term, Dr. McKinney felt the need to retire from active ministry. At the scheduled meeting of the Executive Committee of the West Indies Union, under the supervision of President Israel Leito of the Inter-American Division, I was selected to serve as President of the Union. This also meant that I would be Chair of the Executive Committee, the West Indies College Board, and the Andrews Memorial Hospital Board. Dr. Noel Fraser was invited to serve as the Union's Executive Secretary to fill the now-vacant position I once held. It was good to have Dr. Fraser in this position as a more experienced leader, having held the position of Union President some years before. He was a really comfortable fit in the leadership team, and I can say I benefitted greatly from his experience, wisdom, and comradery.

A well-deserved retirement ceremony was held at the Mandeville Hotel for Dr. Silas McKinney and his beloved wife Ruth, who also retired from her teaching position at the West Indies College, now Northern Caribbean University. They both returned to his native Nassau, Bahamas, to enjoy their well-earned retirement years.

NEW HORIZONS

It was a smooth transition of leadership that enabled us to continue the momentum of development in all aspects of the work in the Union, including inspiring the Conferences to continue full speed with their evangelistic activities. The new team continued to motivate and inspire workers towards reaching the evangelistic goals of the Union, and with that, the Union was able to reach, in 1999, the highest one-year evangelistic record, (a record that has not been broken to the time of writing) of 16,343 new members joining the fellowship of the Seventh-day Adventist community of faith.

I believe that aside from the definite involvement and influence of the Holy Spirit on people's lives, one other factor contributing to this surge in baptism at that time was the international rumor, fear, and speculations of what dire situations would occur with the arrival of the year 2000, known as Y2K. The Y2K Scare was a phenomenon at the turn of the 21st century, when computer users and programmers feared that computers would stop working on **December 31, 1999**. The phenomenon was also referred to as the "Millennium Bug" or "Year 2000 problem" by technology experts. There was also the fear that at midnight on December 31, 1999, computers would go back to 1900 instead of moving forward to the new year 2000. Not only electrical gadgets would not work properly, but there was the strong possibility that life on earth would end as we know it, so what better thing to do with your life than give it to God!? I do not recall any of the computer manufacturers making any effort to allay these fears, except they played upon the fears by marketing "Y2K Compliant Computers." The fact we are here is a clear indicator that none of that happened, but a lesson learned about human behavior was how fear of the unknown can be a great motivator, and when that reason for fear is no longer a threat, people default to business as usual.

So, as the new team settled in, it was not an unreasonable expectation from our constituents to establish new horizons of achievements for the Church's ministry throughout the territory. With much energy in cooperation with the various conferences, we engaged the Union's strategic plan through administrative audits in each field and institution, as we worked closely with them to reach their goals for the rest of the quinquennium.

I consider myself to be fortunate to lead the Union at a time that I could consider as the "golden age" for the church as we had so many positive things going on at the same time. Our University was thriving, our Hospital was growing and becoming more profitable, and our Capital Development Fund was strong and growing as it served the developmental needs of the churches and institutions by providing them loans at concessionary rates on terms that were much more favorable than the commercial banks.

We were able to establish the Workers Loan Fund, which would be funded by the monthly rent assistance given to employees, which became a pool of funds from which employees could get loans for their housing needs at concessionary terms much more favorable than the banks.

INSTITUTIONS OF THE WEST INDIES UNION

As mentioned earlier, one of the things a Union by its constitution is permitted to do is establish tertiary institutions and industries that support the ministry objectives of the organization. These institutions may then establish industries that provide financial support for their mission and provide employment for students who may be on a work-study program. Our philosophy as a church from its inception is that our youth should be educated by teachers who subscribe to the beliefs that guide us as a church. Lack of resources should not be a factor that could deny anyone from accessing such an education, therefore opportunities should be provided for such students to work, save, and pay their way through school in their chosen field of study. So two institutions were created that support this philosophy; the publishing ministry, which allows the student or any member to sell health, gospel books, and magazines and earn funds, as well as Westico Foods, which facilitates students who desire to or must work to pay for their education.

WESTICO FOODS

Westico Foods was a manufacturing entity where health foods were canned, cornflakes were produced as well as a bakery that produced bread and other products. This institution was first established and run by the Inter-American Division Food Company in Miami, with the Division owning 51% share and the West Indies Union, now Jamaica Union Conference, holding 49% share. The factory was cited on the grounds of the then West Indies College, now Northern Caribbean University.

This industry was very welcome as it provided work for students and helped them acquire new skills that many were able to use later in life for great success. Westico Foods experienced periods of ups and downs in its operations. It was in one of those downward spirals that the Inter-American Division decided to exit the management and ownership as it was not considered to be any longer a profitable venture for them.

In December 1996, the Union officers were invited to an urgent meeting at an agreed location in Kingston, with the officers of the Division and the Manager of the IAD Food Company. We were completely unaware of the item on the agenda, but as the meeting opened, we were greeted with the news that the Division had taken the decision to close the Factory with immediate effect, or, if we didn't agree, we could get someone to operate with us on a partnership basis. Of course, this was shocking news to us. Was there any way to salvage this situation? We thought of the many students who depended on employment there to facilitate their "work-study" program. We also thought of the implications to the West Indies College budget.

Before the meeting concluded, the Division officers had made a small concession by giving us thirty to forty-five days from the date to put in effect our decision as their relationship would end.

We had to treat the matter with urgency to determine whether we would operate it ourselves or sell the business to anyone who would operate it on the same basis as the Division did. The Union clearly did not have the expertise to run the business, so we decided to find a partner who could supply the needed management expertise, as that was perceived to be the main problem. We were able to establish an agreement with Scott's Holdings Ltd, an Adventist family from Spanish Town, to purchase a minority share partnership of 49% and join us in operating the business. We were able to invest new funds in the business to restore the factory and purchase new equipment to get it back to a viable state as it was showing signs of aging and greatly reduced usefulness.

The operation showed good signs of progress for a while, but soon was plagued by some of the same ineffi-ciencies, and a strained relationship with the partners led to the eventual closure of the venture. This was a really unfortunate development. When an evaluation was done, it showed that it was no longer considered wise to further invest scarce financial resources into a business that should be bringing in resources to fund aspects of the University's operations and provide "non-tithe revenue" for the mission. The Union Committee voted to cease operations and we all felt the pain of failure and loss.

THE CAPITAL DEVELOPMENT FUND

The Capital Development Fund was a creation of the West Indies Union Conference under the careful and astute management of then treasurer Dr, Aston Barnes. Having drawn inspiration from a similar institution in the United States, Dr. Barnes sought and received approval to develop a Capital Development Fund for the Union. It was not an easy approval process, as we believed the General Conference was not confident it would be managed successfully. But with persistence and purpose, the Union leaders persevered until the approval was secured. When I became the President of the Union, Dr. Barnes continued as my treasurer, and one thing we determined was that this Fund should continue to grow, and fulfill its purpose for the betterment of the churches and institution. The Capital Development Fund until the end of my Administration was so successful that it became a model for other Unions, and our treasurer made several trips to other Unions to explain how we did it.

The Fund's objective was to harness the financial resources of the church organizations and institutions that were in savings accounts in the Banks; plus the reserves that by policy the organizations must maintain, as well as funds that members may wish to deposit. The interest gained through safe investments, like government papers, better-negotiated interest rates with the banks, and internal loans to the organizations and churches, would constitute revenue to the fund. Depositors with a mind for the mission would receive a 2% below commercial rates, and that 2% would also become revenue to the Fund for lending to the institutions and churches to be used for developmental purposes.

This Fund, for years, has been the lifeblood of the Institutions of the Union that would have to pay much higher rates at the banks, and frankly only for those that would qualify. The University and Hospital were great beneficiaries as they could get loans at better than bank rates to purchase equipment and do infrastructure expansion.

The Fund prospered as many mission-minded members and churches became members by making their regular deposits. Unfortunately, following the retirement of Dr, Aston Barnes, the funds were terribly mismanaged and were no longer able to offer the same level of development resources to the Institutions and Churches.

THE PUBLISHING MINISTRY

The Publishing Ministry is another institution operated by the Church through the Union organization. Its purpose is to publish the gospel through the printed pages of religious magazines and health promotional books. This also was structured to help students or any member of the church who does not have a steady source of income or wishes to establish another stream of income, to engage in selling these health-promoting books, Christian magazines, and other materials produced by the ministry.

Individuals who engage in this ministry are called "Colporteurs," who may engage on a full-time or part-time basis. Those who engage with the objective of gaining funds to continue their academic pursuit would do so, especially in the summertime, to achieve these scholarships and are classified as "Student Colporteurs." I was one such "Student Colporteur" during my time of study at West Indies College. I was able to travel to Toronto, Canada, during the summer of 1975 along with my friend Dr. Gladstone Knight in search of and was successful in gaining our scholarships that year. As a married student with one salary in the house, I had to work in order to pay my school fees. I worked at the bakery 16 hours per week, sold books in Jamaica for a summer, two summers in Canada, and spent one summer in Kingston doing real estate sales with another friend and fellow student, Pastor Claude Brown.

Numerous individuals who have held, and others who are still holding, important positions of power and influence in the church structure, as well as in politics, industry, commerce, and society in general were able to complete their academic program up to graduate level by paying their way through having gained summer scholarships. Many members have been able to sustain themselves, educate their children, and support their families through this ministry. No member of the Seventh-day Adventist Church who is willing to work should end up on the welfare list of the church or the country, at least in our Western democracies. There is a way out through the Publishing Ministry of the Church!

With the development of the internet marketing of books, the program is somewhat modified, but hard copies of books and magazines are still being bought, so the fact still holds true.

ANDREWS MEMORIAL HOSPITAL

One of the oldest health institutions on the Island of Jamaica, which still continues to hold pride of place by offering outstanding medical services to the country and region, is the Andrews Memorial Hospital, situated at 27 Hope Road in Kingston 10. It was my privilege to be not only a Hospital Board member for several years but to also serve as its Board Chair for three years.

Brief History

In 1943, the General Conference of Seventh-day Adventists and the officers of the Inter-American Division realized that some form of medical work should be started in the Division. Dr. Clifford Russell Anderson was approached and invited to commence this work. In March 1944, the property at 27 Hope Road, Kingston, Jamaica was purchased. Towards the end of 1944, the first doctor and the first nurse for the Inter-American Division arrived in Jamaica. In April 1945, the erection of the clinic building commenced, and by the end of the year, it was in functioning order with the help of E. E. Walters for the Pharmacy, Mr. Crooks in the Laboratory, and Misses Lena Henriques and Ellice Hogg in the Social Service Department. Also in 1945, Miss Ruth Munroe started lecturing in pre-nursing subjects at the West Indian Training College. The official opening of the clinic took place on December 12, 1945. Toward the end of 1946, a ground-breaking ceremony for the proposed new hospital building took place. [1]

Andrews Hospital was one of the Mission Hospitals of the Church that are established around the world. The objective of these mission hospitals is to share the gospel through the encouragement of a healthy lifestyle that benefits the mental, social, emotional, and spiritual aspects of our being. The philosophy of the health ministry is to model the healing ministry of Christ and not primarily to be a competitor to any established health institution. We believe, however, that our health Institutions should offer the best care found anywhere through the combined use of science and natural medical procedures to bring healing to the whole being.

In the early days, the medical staff and sometimes nurses were expatriates supplied through the General Conference. They would bring with them their various expertise and would link with other overseas Adventist hospitals to facilitate best practices.

The Andrews Hospital enjoys an excellent reputation in Kingston for offering the best nursing care to its patients. Other services offered by the hospital continue to be of high quality and well-recognized. It was so well thought of, that on April 7, 1982, when President Ronald Reagan and his wife Nancy visited Jamaica, Andrews Hospital was selected as the Hospital of choice for the President should there be any emergency occurring during his visit. There was none, but the fact that Andrews was chosen speaks volumes about its position in Jamaica at the time.

Today, the Hospital is the only institution in Jamaica that processes medicals for people intending to migrate to the United States. This was achieved, not by application, but by invitation of the United States Embassy in Jamaica, and that also speaks volumes regarding the confidence factor regarding the integrity of the reports rendered.

Mr. Astor & Mrs. Novelette Tai were very generous benefactors of the Hospital and also provided financing for the expansion of a wing of the hospital. The wing was dedicated to their memory, and known as the "The Aston & NoveletteTai Wing." Here's a report on the dedication of the wing as reported by Nigel Coke, Communication Director of the Jamaica Union:

"Andrews Memorial Hospital, owned and operated by the Seventh-day Adventist Church in the West Indies region, officially opened its new wing in its Kingston, Jamaica, facility on Sep. 27. During the inaugural ceremony, His Excellency, Governor General Sir Howard Cooke, officially declared the new wing (The Tai Wing) opened after a dedication and thanksgiving service held at the Andrews Memorial Seventh-day Adventist Church nearby. Hospital and church administrators were present to renew their commitment to providing medical service to the community in its 61st year.

During the inaugural ceremony, Mr. Randy Haffner, senior vice president and chief operating officer at Florida Hospital, congratulated and gave an award to hospital and church administrators.

The new wing will house 11 doctors' offices on the ground floor, 15 medical/surgical beds on the first floor, and a 12-bed obstetrics unit on the second floor. The hospital also houses the only epilepsy center with Video EEG in the English-speaking Caribbean.

Andrews Memorial Hospital has been offering high-quality medical service for the community since it opened in 1944."

Governor General Honorable Howard Cooke (L) and Dr. Patrick Allen, (R) President of Jamaica Union Conference of S D A. (Allen currently serves as Governor General of Jamaica)

NORTHERN CARIBBEAN UNIVERSITY (WEST INDIES COLLEGE)

Brief History

Northern Caribbean University is a private, liberal arts institution owned and operated by the Jamaica Union Conference (JAMU) and the Atlantic Caribbean Union Mission (ACUM) of Seventh-day Adventists, and is located in Jamaica. With its main campus only 2 miles south of Mandeville town, in Manchester, and three other campuses situated in Kingston, Montego Bay, and Salem Runaway Bay, St. Ann, this university offers a number of professional, pre-professional, and vocational programs in a spiritually wholesome and aesthetically pleasing atmosphere.

Northern Caribbean University is the oldest private tertiary institution in Jamaica and was first known as West Indian Training School. It began with 8 students in 1907, as an institution offering courses only up to the twelfth grade. Following a temporary closure in 1913, it resumed operations in 1919. In 1936 it was renamed West Indian Training College. As its offerings developed to include theology, teacher education, secretarial science, business, and natural sciences, it became a junior college. It achieved senior college status in the late 1950s when it began to offer the bachelor's degree in Theology and was renamed West Indies College in 1959. Since then, baccalaureate programs in some twenty other disciplines have been added.

It was while I served as Chairman of the Board in 1999, with Dr. Herbert Thompson as President, that the college, having successfully gained approval for several of its degree programs, was granted university status by the University Council of Jamaica. We convened a College Board meeting in the East Jamaica Conference Board room to, among other agenda items, choose a name for the new University. Several suggestions were proffered, and we finally had a consensus on one name and voted to rename the institution "Northern Caribbean University." Currently, the university offers graduate and post-graduate programs in sciences, religion, business, and education.

The University has made and continues to make a significant impact on the academic landscape of not only Jamaica but the region and the world. The university gained global exposure in the Microsoft Imagine Cup competition of 2007 where members of the Computer and Information Sciences department competing as Team ICAD took 3rd place.

NCU was crowned regional champion in 2005, 2007, and 2009. In 2007, NCU Imagine Cup Team (ICAD) represented Jamaica and the region at the world finals in South Korea, where they outclassed competitors from across the globe to place 3rd in the world. This performance speaks volumes for the quality of the University's academic offerings, and the vigilance of a forward-looking Board of Governors.

Gaining University status in 1999 unleashed a positive burst of energy, enthusiasm, and pride that stimulated its benefactors and visionary President Dr. Herbert Thompson to develop the physical infrastructure, and the enrolment increased at a rapid pace. My chairmanship of the Board was a brief 3-year stint as in the year 2000, at the General Conference Session, I was invited to serve the church at the regional level, which occasioned the relocation of my family to Miami, Florida.

The University continues to make a significant impact in the academic and scientific landscape of Jamaica and beyond. The latest development to emerge from the science department of the University was the discovery of special nutraceutical and medicinal elements in a ginger-like plant discovered in Jamaica. The product is now being marketed worldwide as "Zon Teasan," a premium blend of tea known for its nutraceutical and health-promoting value.

School song: Alma Mater
Word: Herbert John Thompson
Song: Daniel Rodriquez

To the blessed hill you brought us
Where we've had our hopes and dreams fulfilled.
Oh the glorious things you taught us
'Midst the pine trees and the wind
We will rise and call you blessed
As we strive to serve mankind.

And we'll praise our God each moment
For the love in you we find.
And we'll praise our God each moment
For the love in you we find.

Chorus
Oh dear beacon on the hill
A bastion so true
We pledge our love and loyalty
In gratitude to you.
March onward ever upward, ever forward
Alma Mater, NCU

5
GENERAL CONFERENCE OF SEVENTH-DAY ADVENTISTS

Aerial view of the General Conference of Seventh-day Adventists offices in Maryland USA

The General Conference of Seventh-day Adventists is the coordinating body of the denomination. Located in Silver Spring, Maryland, in the United States, it coordinates the ministries and activities of the Seventh-day Adventist Church worldwide. The Church ascribes to what is described as a "Representative" form of governance. Authority in the Adventist Church stems from church members who select leaders to represent them. Under this representative style of governance, members vote for their choice of personnel to represent them at local, regional, and world levels. The General Conference (GC) is overseen by an elected executive committee and president. As the administrative hub of the Adventist denomination, the GC coordinates efforts to articulate policy and doctrine within the Adventist Church.

Officers of the General Conference are elected at the General Conference Session every five years, or by the GC Executive Committee if needed. At the time of writing, the leading officers of the General Conference are Pastor Ted Wilson, President since 2010, who grew up in Egypt to Missionary parents, Pastor Erton Kohler, Secretary since 2022, who hails from Brazil, and Mr. Paul Douglas, Treasurer since 2022, who hails from Jamaica. [1]

THE GENERAL CONFERENCE SESSION

What is a General Conference Session?

It is the official world meeting of the General Conference of Seventh-day Adventists, held every five years. At the session, delegates from around the world elect the Church's World Leaders, discuss and vote on changes to the Church's Constitution, and listen to reports from the Church's 13 Divisions on activities going on within its territory.

The first session was held on May 20, 1863, in Battle Creek, Michigan with 20 delegates in attendance. The early sessions were held every year in a small church. As the Church's membership grew, the time between sessions lengthened, meeting places got bigger, and more delegates attended. Today, the sessions are held every five years in cities with stadiums that can seat more than 70,000 attendees, which includes the more than 2,400 delegates attending. Visitors from around the world also watch the session on various media. Wikipedia.

OFFICIAL STATEMENTS AND DOCUMENTS

From time to time, the Church takes an official position on various issues, and social and current affairs, which are also voted by the delegates of the session. These statements can be found on the Church's official website at adventist.org/statements.

Many times some people mistakenly take the position that because we believe in the separation of church and state, we should avoid speaking out on social or political issues. But if you choose to investigate, you will find that the church has taken official positions on a wide variety of issues over the years. For example, issues such as: Affirmation of Creation, Global Poverty, War in Congo, Commitment to Health and Healing, Ending Violence against Women and Girls, Homosexuality, Transgenderism, Immunization, Consensus Statement on Seventh-day Adventist Theology of Ordination, etc.

These position statements are usually discussed, refined, and voted at a General Conference Session to reflect the consensus of a worldwide delegation, and should be useful to the church and society on a global basis.

INTER-AMERICAN DIVISION OF SEVENTH-DAY ADVENTISTS

The Inter-American Division is one of thirteen world divisions of the worldwide Seventh-day Adventist Church. It is through these "Divisions" that the General Conference maintains its presence around the world. Rather than giving administrative direction from its headquarters in Silver Springs, Maryland, regional leaders who are generally familiar with the politics, languages, cultures, and traditions in the various regions, are chosen to administer the church's affairs and interact with Governments on behalf of the General Conference. Therefore, the full name of these "Divi-sions" is chosen to reflect the region it is designed to administer. For example, the one that administers our region is "The General Conference Inter-American Division of Seventh-day Adventists," which highlights the geographical location between the North and South Americas.

The divisional structure has proven itself invaluable to the mission of the church, as countries with national political philosophies opposed to the United States system of government, generally find the church's presence and work less objectionable when the church management is in the hands of local/regional leadership.

ESTABLISHMENT OF THE INTER-AMERICAN DIVISION

In 1879, Pastor John N Loughborough – an Adventist missionary from the United States of America who was residing in Southampton, England – and Willian Ings – a colporteur in the same city – sent a box of books to Haiti with no specific addressee. The literature reached the hands of an Episcopalian missionary, who in turn shared the literature with other protestant missionaries. A Baptist missionary distributed the publications within his congregation. When Henry Williams and his wife – a young Jamaican couple in the congregation – studied the literature, they began keeping the Sabbath as a day of rest and began sharing with others what they had learned. In 1892, after more than ten years, Pastor L. C. Chadwick visited them for the first time. He baptized them, and they then became the first Seventh-day Adventists in the Inter-American Division.

Henry Williams and his wife continued their evangelistic activities across Jamaica upon their return from Haiti, and their influence spread throughout the Caribbean region. There were people on other Islands and in other countries who also participated in evangelistic visitation and literature distribution. This contributed to the rapid growth of Adventism in the territory. As the membership grew, the General Conference provided leadership for the work in the territory with (what became) the West Indies Union Conference, which was created in 1906. Subsequently, the Northern Latin American Mission was created in 1914. In 1922, the General Conference organized the Inter-American Division with 8,146 members in 221 churches distributed among three conferences and ten missions. By 1924, the membership in Inter-America had grown to 11,670 members worshipping in 229 churches. It reached a membership of 3.6 million by 2012 and the growth continues today. A primary factor of this growth is the evangelistic visitation carried out by the laity. [2]

The Inter-American Division established its first administrative headquarters in New York, then moved to New Orleans, and then to Cuba before settling in Coconut Grove, Coral Gables, and then Kendall, its current location in Miami, Florida. In a brief interview with Dr. Israel Leito, who gave this history, he also related that since the leaders then were still domiciled in the US, it was good to be established near a port, as the chief means of transportation was by boat at the time. When air travel became more popular, Miami would prove to be most convenient to reach all countries in the territory within a few hours without changing planes.

Today the Division is comprised of 42 countries in the Caribbean, Mexico, and Central America, and five countries in the Northern part of the South American continent, washed by the waters of the Caribbean Sea. With 3.6 million members, the Inter-American Division is one of the most populous divisions of the world field at the time of writing. There are roughly 22,000 Adventist churches in the 24 Unions of this division, which is home to a population of nearly 280 million.

The Division is home to 13 Adventist universities. The region also operates 13 major hospitals, located in Belize, Curacao, Dominican Republic, Guyana, Haiti, Honduras, Jamaica, Puerto Rico, Trinidad, Venezuela, and three in Mexico.

Other major organizations within this division include the Inter-American Adventist Theological Seminary, which offers graduate-level religious education to pastors and teachers on the campus of 10 affiliated Adventist universities and seminaries. Adventist Health Services in IAD serves as an association of all the Seventh-day Adventist healthcare institutions in the division. In an effort to share the gospel throughout the region, IAD oversees nine media centers, seven radio stations, and numerous Internet radio ministries. [3]

There are four principal languages which are English, Spanish, French, and Dutch through which the Division carries out its work in the territory.

Divisions of the General Conference, unlike the Unions and Conferences, have no constituency of members but are all governed by the policies of the General Conference for that region. In fact, while there are five functional levels constituting the church structure, there are only four constituent levels. The Division provides leadership and policy guidelines to those Unions within its designated territory.

All officers of the Division are elected by the delegates of the General Conference in session every five years and are considered Associates of their counterparts at the General Conference. For example, the President of the Division is also a Vice President of the General Conference. Usually, during the time of the General Conference Session, a nominating committee representing all the Unions and their institutions in that region is chosen to elect other officers and directors as needed to administer the work of the church in any particular region. Some Divisions choose to return to their territory and conduct this activity, which is quite permissible as it facilitates greater participation of local leadership and membership, and is certainly more cost-effective.

The operating policies that govern the Unions and Conferences are amended, updated, or modified annually as the needs arise by vote of the General Conference at its annual Council. These amendments are then voted on and accepted at the lower levels of the organizational structure to formalize the adaptation of the policies which will subsequently become their policies.

With regards to the Constitution of each entity, it is important to observe that each can be modified to fit into local situations, but only sections in "light prints" can be modified locally and all sections in "Bold prints" can be modified only by vote of the larger/higher entity.

If a local/lower organization sees the need for any modification of the "Bold Prints," such an organization may request such modification through a vote of its governing Committee and send it to the Division Committee for processing. This would be studied and if such modification is found to be beneficial to the entire territory, then it is voted and implemented. Occasionally, there are members who think the structure is too "involved" and express the desire to eliminate one or more levels, but this idea has never found traction, because to this point it is found to be of great value in keeping a worldwide organization such as ours united and functioning effectively.

MY CALL TO SERVE AT THE INTER-AMERICAN DIVISION

It was in the last week of June of the year 2000 that, as delegates from the West Indies Union, we boarded our flight from the Norman Manley International Airport in Kingston to beautiful Toronto International Airport for the opening of the 57th General Conference Session of the world church under the theme "Almost Home," with 1,844 officially accredited delegates from 201 countries around the world.

Once the delegates were seated at the opening session, they each received a large 3-ring agenda notebook including documents to be discussed and voted on. Each business session is chaired by a General Conference (GC) vice president and secretary who guided the discussions. Delegates vote on policies and amendments placed before them and also have the option of speaking to issues from the floor before official adoption.

At a previously scheduled Business Session, the Nominating Committee was established to elect the officers and directors of the General Conference office. Since as stated before, the Divisions are Divisions of the General Conference, elections of its officials are due at this time as well, so the three Officers of each world division are usually elected by the same Nominating Committee. Some Divisions choose to Caucus and do their elections for Directors at the general session, and the Inter-American Division is one such, while others choose to hold their Sessions soon thereafter within their respective regions.

It was at this Caucus Session I was invited to serve as Vice President of the Inter-American region, which was voted by the delegates from our Division territory. Thus, began my last 17 years of service at the Division headquarters in Miami, Florida.

SERVING IN THE INTER-AMERICAN DIVISION

Upon arriving at the Division, I, along with the other newcomers, attended the orientation session that was organized to familiarize us with the roles we were expected to perform, and the assignment of portfolios that we would carry. In addition to my role as Vice President, I was asked to be responsible for setting the dates for all Union & Conference Sessions to be held in the Division, the "INHOUSE" operations, be Secretary of

Adventist Laymen Services and Industries (ASI), and be the Divisions´ representative to International Children's Care Int. (ICC) located in Washington State, but operates in 7 children's villages in the countries of Guatemala, Dominican Republic, Mexico, El Salvador, and Nicaragua, all within our Division territory.

This organization is a Lay-lead ministry that developed out of the severe devastation that resulted from a deadly 7.5 magnitude earthquake that hit Guatemala City on February 4, 1976, at 3:01 am, which resulted in a high death toll of 23,000 persons. Approximately 76,000 were injured, and over 1.2 million people rendered homeless.

Among the homeless were thousands of children who became orphaned as a result of this catastrophe; and then Union President, Pastor Robert Folkenberg, invited Pastor Fleck and his wife to help by coming up with a plan on how the church could help. Thus, began the International Children's Care ministry which has gone global. The organization is also a member of ASI International.

My association with International Children's Care was and continues to be an inspiration, that led me to establish the Educational Foundation for Children's Care Inc. to care for homeless, abandoned, abused, and neglected children at our facility in Clarendon, Jamaica. The Foundation also supports children of incarcerated people and offers scholarships to needy children of minority populations in South Florida, where I presently reside.

The work of the Educational Foundation closely

mirrors that of ICC, having established a MOU, the Foundation was accepted as an affiliate of the International Children's Care Inc.

ADVENTIST LAYMEN SERVICES & INDUSTRIES (ASI)

The Adventist Laymen Services & Industries (ASI) is an organization consisting of Seventh-day Adventist Business and Professional laypersons. They are members who have a passion for the mission and seek to supplement the organized Church with personnel, skills, and resources to enhance its mission.

Of necessity, there must be continuing close collaboration between ASI and the church, and to ensure this bond remains strong, the ASI reserves the position of Secretary/Treasurer, or Secretary or Treasurer as one to be filled only by a full-time worker of the church. This was the position I was asked to fill as successor to Pastor Gordon Martinborough, the first Secretary of ASI Inter-America. I came in at a time when the organization was in its infancy in the Division.

I was first introduced to ASI by laymen Fitz Henry, Errol Long, Dr. Anthony Frankson, et al, who had organized ASI in Kingston, East Jamaica, while I served in the Central Jamaica Conference. The fledgling organization grew to the extent that when the Inter-American Division ASI decided to hold its inaugural convention in 1999, they chose Kingston, Jamaica because there was this fledgling group to work with.

This convention brought together delegates from the

various English, Spanish, and French-speaking coun-tries of the region. It was a very successful convention under the leadership of its first president, Mr. George Piper, a native of Antigua & Barbuda, and Pastor Martin-borough, the first Secretary.

My introduction to the organization put me in good stead to learn more and give leadership to this organi-zation at the Division level as Secretary. Without a doubt, the first convention became the template for growing and expanding the organization throughout the division. During my tenure, I was able with the committee to execute 15 conventions in 10 countries of our division. The ASI continues to be strong and active throughout the territory, which for me is a very satis-fying outcome. Maintaining chapter viability across the region in the various language groups was a great chal-lenge, but to the extent, we were able to train our lead-ers, and with the support of organizational leaders in the field, we can count this a real success. I will be forever grateful for the collaboration and friendships we developed as we work together with these dedi-cated, highly motivated professionals and business people.

INHOUSE OPERATIONS

As its nomenclature indicates, this is a committee that oversees and approves any structural modification and use of the building, maintenance of its facilities and grounds. This includes determining the office space to be used by incoming personnel, janitorial services, terms of use of the auditorium, making it available to be used as a polling station at election times as a public good etc.

Any activity that requires the expenditure of funds would of necessity be a recommendation to Administration for further consideration and approval.

MY FIRST ASSIGNMENT

My first trip as Vice President was to the Country of Haiti. This came with much trepidation, because it would be to a French-speaking country, and I had no knowledge of French at all, as opposed to my limited knowledge of Spanish, though I could not make a sentence. I was relieved when my friend Dr Eli Honore, a Haitian native I met when as classmates we pursued the Master of Science in Public Health (MSPH) degree, offered then by Loma Linda University, decided to accompany me to provide translation and other support.

The trip went very well and nothing near the trepidation I felt prior to going. One reason was that I was able to find Pastors who were graduates of West Indies College (Now Northern Caribbean University), who spoke English and were happy to receive me and made my visit a memorable one. One such was the Union President Pastor Edzer Obas. He and his wife were the most gracious hosts who entertained us for Sabbath lunches etc.

As appointments began to roll in, I quickly realized I had to step up my game in learning at least one other language well. I decided on Spanish. Spanish was my language of choice from very early on. My grandfather,

James Sparks, was one of those who worked in Cuba for some time, and upon his return would mesmerize us with his newly acquired language, and used to tune the radio to listen to Spanish stations originating in the neighboring Island of Cuba. I decided then I needed to know what they were saying because it seemed fun as he would laugh at what must have been Spanish comedy. So, when my Primary School principal introduced the subject, I was one of his eager students and found the language fascinating.

Now, being at the Division and the majority of Unions being Spanish, the need to be fluent was great, to say the least. With an eight-week intensive course and some practice, I was able to develop more confidence in serving the largest language group of the Division with some degree of efficiency and confidence. It was always gratifying to see how appreciative the other language groups were when I attempted to communicate in their mother tongue. They would assure me that the errors I made were not fatal, as they understood my message.

IAD COMMUNICATION DEPARTMENT

In 2002, I was asked by our President Leito to assume leadership of the Communication Department of the Division for what I thought would be a temporary appointment to complete the term, consequent to the resignation after two years of the Session appointed Director. Now I know better.

It was also a critical time for the Department. It was during this time that our Department was experiencing an evolution in that we were still dependent upon paper reports coming in from the fields. We were now about to transition to electronic reports and also to embark upon video production for broadcast on the electronic media that was being developed now known as Hope Channel. The communication director who completed the previous term, Doctor L. V. Macmillan, had already begun setting the template by establishing production centers at selected educational institutions. I was given an assistant director, in the person of Brother Jose Romero, who was then our IT technician in the office at the time. We began working as a team, with his technical skills while I concentrated on much of the propaganda and promotional aspects, following the crafting of a vision for the Department.

One of the early things we did was to promote the establishment of downlink centers in all our churches throughout the Division. Our Division provided subsidies in order to accomplish this goal. We consider this to have been a very successful execution, but that was only part of what we needed to do. Providing downlink centers without programs that reflect our region appeared to be counterproductive. The next move, therefore, was to produce programs with which our people could identify. For this, our division also provided subsidies to the educational institutions to assist with program production. Two institutions were selected for this project, one in English-speaking territory, which is the Northern Caribbean University in Jamaica, and the other in Spanish-speaking territory, which is the Montemorelos University in Mexico. The reason these two universities were selected was that they had fully developed Media Departments where students receive practical experiences in pre and post-production, script writing, and even become actors themselves. It also made a lot more sense to support these Institutions by having them produce programs that could be aired on satellite television, which also meant that equipment had to be at industry standards, so our Division also made the required investments.

LIVE PRODUCTIONS

It was also at this time that our division launched into live satellite production of programs from the field. This was a real breakthrough because it was not done before, so we had no template to follow. It was quite cumbersome and costly to pack boxes and boxes of equipment and shipped by air to various locations. Brother Romero was instrumental in designing a portable production studio and incorporating the use of a Tricaster, which we were able to ship much easier to various locations to more conveniently produce live programming. This was a breakthrough for our department and for this, I am eternally grateful to our leadership at the Division level, who were willing to support our vision of possibilities for our department and much was accomplished.

Another thing we discovered was that, while there was a need for new programming, there was no consistent way of supporting the production. I soon learned that production for television is a very expensive proposition, so we developed a plan by which all our entities would be required to make a provision of .5% of their income, to support the training of staff and also the production of programs to be broadcast on Hope Channel. This we developed and the financial plan was voted on by the division committee, and while some organizations struggled with the idea, many embraced it and reserved that portion and more in their budgets. They were now envisioning the awesome possibilities that satellite evangelism could do for their fields. The churches already had the infrastructure of downlink centers, and the union and conference leaders were now ready to do programming that reflected their culture and language to be broadcast locally and internationally.

Our team at the Division and other specialists that we could muster logged many hours in training and developing the skills of our collaborators in the field, which includes both directors and technical personnel in the respective territories.

It became obvious that the two of us could no longer cope with the demands and the needs in the field. It was also at this time that the Communication industry was changing from analog to digital broadcasts. We needed skills that I didn't have in digital media, so it was at this time the division tapped a very able Professor Abel Marquez, then serving at Montemorelos University, to become Assistant Communication Director for the Division. Professor Abel was a tremendous and valuable addition to the team, and together we traveled the territory for many of these training sessions and program production.

THE WEBSITE AND TRANSITION

We also took on the challenge of developing a website for the Division that would carry news from the headquarters of actions voted to be implemented in the field, evangelistic activities, developments in our educational and health institutions, and news from the wider organizations and from the world in general. We engaged remote translators to help with getting the news out in a timely manner, as news is news when it is new!

This development required someone who could devote more time to acquiring and organizing the incoming news, as well as the news from the headquarters. So, we expressed our need for such assistance to the administration, and soon we were welcoming aboard Libna Stevens to the communications team as our News Editor and Writer. Libna was a valuable addition as she brought to the team her bilingual strength and excellent writing skills.

Over the years, our innovative and talented team functioned like a well-oiled machinery. It became the No. 1 source in the General Conference for the production of newsworthy items for publication and broadcast, and was highly recognized and commended by the World Church.

Together as a team we were able to set the template for communication activities for the new millennium which continues to evolve on an ever-increasing rapid pace.

As a consequence, and for the closing of this chapter of my service, my able, knowledgeable, and affable associate, Abel Marquez, was selected to fill the gap, which he has done well and has continued the pace without skipping a beat. One thing I appreciated about my team was the great spirit of harmony, diligence, creativity, and collaboration, which characterized our relationship and work.

SPIRIT OF PROPHECY & RESEARCH CENTERS

To the uninitiated, the term "Spirit of Prophecy" could be a real puzzle. The term Spirit of Prophecy refers to the work of the Holy Spirit in the guiding and recording of various spiritual activities that demonstrate more clearly who God is and interprets His will for humanity since the entrance of sin.

Another terminology associated with this theme is the "Gift of Prophecy." The Gift is precisely what it sounds like – a gift. It is not a gift that one can pray for, study for or work to attain. This gift comes not from the generosity of any human being but is divinely given to one or more human beings whom God alone chooses. It is a "gift" that God gives to anyone He chooses during the length and breadth of human history, specifically for the purpose that the person so chosen should become God's mouthpiece to His "church " in particular, and with a message for humanity in general.

Bible writers are all examples of human beings who have received the "gift" from God to interpret God's messages and will for humanity. It also foretells future events that would impact the church and/or the world, with the intent that mankind should make the necessary preparations to receive such predicted events. An example of this is the foretelling of the return of Jesus Christ to earth in **Luke 21:25-28**. Mankind needs to make the preparation now if he/she chooses to be with Christ then, and consequently escape the horrific conflagration predicted for the conclusion of human history on this earth.

The Seventh-day Adventist Church acknowledges that there is no predicted termination to the end to influence the "Spirit of Prophecy," so it is safe to conclude that the prophetic ministry of the Spirit will continue to guide the Church until the end of time. In the same way, the influence of "the gift" within the church will continue to be manifested until the end of time.

Based upon the application of generally accepted biblical tests applied to anyone claiming to have received the prophetic call, Seventh-day Adventists believe that Ellen White, who became a founding member of the church, was a beneficiary of that call. Her subsequent display of that "gift" has proven to be a blessing to the Church. Her ministry can be credited to a great extent to the worldwide unity of the message, practices, and mission focus of the denomination. Her extensive writings for the guidance of the early Advent believers have caused her to be listed among the world's most famous and prolific writers.

There was a real need for the guidance that this gift provided at a critical time in the development of a new movement, and that eventually became the Seventh-day Adventist church. The group of Advent believers was comprised of people who were members of the existing churches of the day. They remained members of their respective congregations until their focus and agitation regarding the imminent return of Christ became too unbearable, and they were eventually disfellowshipped.

Another challenge for the new believers was the wide spectrum of beliefs among them. How would these beliefs be reconciled? The only thing they seemed to have had in common was their conviction that the "second coming of Christ" was imminent. This was the place where the prophetic gift played a critical role in doctrinal development, eventually unifying this disparate group. This unity was not an easily nor quickly achieved goal, but eventually, over time, as egos gave way to surrender, the illusive doctrinal unity became a reality.

Considering the timeless nature of Ellen White's messages, counsels, and guidance, it is considered important that they be preserved for future generation of believers to access and examine for themselves. Before her death, Ellen White established a board of trustees, consisting of leading members of the General Conference, to become custodians of her manuscripts, pay any debt remaining, and publish materials, as thought appropriate for the church, after her death.

The Ellen G. White Estate is that organization, which continues to carry that mandate according to the guidelines she gave then. This organization is not a department of the General Conference, it operates independently and appoints members to fill any vacancy that may arise on its board. Members of the church or members of the public who wish to do research on Ellen White's ministry, or any theme or counsel she gave, can have access to all of the resources of the Estate at the main office in Washington or any of the Resource Centers located around the world.

As the Church continued to grow, it became necessary for more of our members to be exposed to the history and works of this important pioneering member of our organization. The first Research center was established by the White Estate outside of the United States, on the campus of the Montemorelos University in Mexico, which facilitates the Spanish speaking members who wish to have access to the holdings of the Estate. All the materials in the principal office are faithfully and electronically copied and placed in the centers. Since then, several others have been established worldwide, and under my watch we were to get another established in our Division, on the campus of the Northern Caribbean University in Mandeville, Jamaica, to serve the Caribbean area.

As technology develops, there may no longer be the need for the establishment of physical Research Centers as they presently operate, but instead a new paradigm that utilizes the resources that are now available online, which are published and maintained by the White Estate at whiteestate.org. This project is almost complete at the time of writing.

One of my most satisfying achievements in this ministry was to have the entire nine volumes of the Testimonies translated into French for the first time. This important language group in our territory was now able to read, for themselves, in their own language, these inspired counsels for Godly living.

I was able to advance the objectives of this ministry through the conducting of scores of weekend seminars and leadership workshops. We were able to do so in all four major languages of the Division. The workshops and seminars are usually well-attended or even over-flowing, and feedback was usually very positive as we were able to clear up much of the misinformation and doubts through the presentations and Q&As. These weekend seminars were structured to educate and inform, and were obviously well appreciated.

COUNTRIES I HAVE VISITED

Working in the Division as a Vice President gives one the opportunity to travel to various countries for assignments and appointments. Especially in the case of the Inter-American Division, which geographically is in another Division territory. Some, however, may be surprised to know that at the time of the establishment of the Inter-American Division, the General Conference Committee voted that its territory would include the lower part of Florida and the south of West Palm Beach to the Cays. While it remains a voted action, it was never implemented. If that were implemented, then the Division office would be within its assigned territory. I would posit that the decision to situate the office in Miami was a well-thought-out one, as every appointment to serve the region requires an airline ticket, and Miami has the most convenient airport that serves the region. One flight can get you to any country of the territory within a day, whereas if the offices of the Division were located elsewhere, it would require taking at least two aircrafts, with a necessary stopover in Miami anyway. In addition, were it not in Miami, there could be possible complications arising from visa issues for some personnel. One can easily see how the transportation cost factor would become a very expensive proposition.

In addition to those service calls, there were activities outside the Division's territory to which one was invited. For many months, a Division officer could be gone from home for three of four weeks. I have known of times when there was only enough time between flights to exchange suitcases for a prepacked one to continue a journey.

My extraterritorial trips have taken me to Canada, Brazil, Argentina, Ecuador, Malawi, South Africa, Egypt, Jordan, Qatar, Dubai, Philippines, Thailand, Greece, Switzerland, France, Netherlands, Germany, Italy, Israel, Japan, China, South Korea, England, Spain, and Turkey. I have learned a lot from these visits and interactions, as I observe my church in operation within cultures and political systems so different from ours. Only a God who actively controls the destiny of His church could keep this organization so united, cogent, coherent, and relevant, saving it from fragmentation into regional independent entities.

6

REALITY CHECK

RETIREMENT AND ITS AFTERMATH

After forty exciting years of ministry and a seemingly endless travel schedule, the time had now come to hang up the proverbial hat of active engagement and support the ministry from the Grandstand with occasional intervention on the field of play. June 30, 2017, was the historic day I left the premises of the Inter-American Division as an active employee and entered upon the yet unknown but anticipated life of retirement. Soon, I began to explore what retirees do when they wake up the following morning without an agenda. To be honest, the first day at home felt so weird! Not having to rush the breakfast and the traffic to get to worship at the office on time was strange but appreciated. One new idea developed, which would involve the writing of this volume to chronicle my experience with the hope that some part of my life experience would inspire my grandkids and help others to aspire and persevere.

My wife needed to work for a few more months to qualify for denominational pension benefits, so I was indeed alone at home. Thankfully, that would only be a temporary situation. Now I was the one preparing snacks for her lunch at work, and anxiously awaiting her return. Now the shoe was squarely on the other foot! I made dinner so she could come home, have a hot meal, and relax.

As time went by, I found there were many personal and family-related matters that were unattended due to my previously busy travel schedule.

I also found time to be more engaged with activities surrounding my alma mater, Northern Caribbean University, as well as my charitable organization, Educational Foundation for Children's Care Inc.

It is amazing how life does not always follow one's preferred script. Our ideas about retirement were to use the time to visit family, friends, and interesting places we might have missed or gone, but never had the time to enjoy. Take the occasional cruise, do leadership training/workshop, and do other things along the line of my preparation, all, of course, at my discretion and timeline.

Unfortunately, these and other plans we had were short-lived, or better experienced "stillbirth," because, in only a few months, we were to receive an unexpected and rather devastating diagnosis for my wife that turned everything upside down.

Apparently, there was another agenda of which we

were unaware; but as it unfolded, I was compelled to put mine on hold and accept this radically changed agenda.

Within the first six months of Shirnet's retirement, and a year of mine, I discovered that she was not coping as well as she was accustomed to doing with the daily chores, those easy tasks that I knew she would expertly dispatch. I realized she was asking the same question repeatedly, which was unusual. Honestly, before I became concerned, I was more than a little annoyed with the repeated interrogation, only to realize she had no recollection of either asking the question or receiving any answers.

My first awareness that something was radically wrong, was one night we were sitting on the bed attending separate issues. I noticed she was counting some United States currency, as well as Jamaican bills, and was experiencing real difficulty. It was not that many bills, so that raised my concern. As a past "A level" economics High School teacher, if Shirnet was having difficulty counting money, then this is a real problem. I took some time to observe out of the corner of my eyes what was taking place, until she said to me, "Leon, I don't know what is happening, but I cannot seem to count these bills," so I offered to help. I discovered she was mixing both currencies and even so, could not tabulate the same.

PHYSICIAN'S INTERVENTIONS

It was then I realized that her inability to cope with her usual tasks could be a sign of something deeper that was going on and not just tiredness. The repeating of herself in an ordinary conversation was becoming more frequent, so we decided to consult her primary care physician.

I shared with him my observations and the events of concern. He decided to send my wife for a battery of tests to discover what might be the causal factors of her apparent cognitive decline.

When the test results were analyzed, he decided to refer her to a Neurology Specialist for his professional evaluation. We were soon onto another series of tests and medications, while her situation seemed to be on a rapid downward spiral. She became less able to focus on customarily routine domestic activities, and during this time of perplexity came another complicating factor.

Her eldest brother, who lived an hour away from us, became severely ill, and so we visited as we would on occasions. Upon leaving his home that evening, Shirnet asked what I thought about his condition. I volunteered my honest opinion that I did not think he would last much longer, which did not land very well, as that appeared to be an unexpected, negative response. So, as we drove home, I tried to soften the effect of my response, but I noticed she was reflecting deeply on all that transpired that evening. In less than a week we received the expected call which informed us that Llewelyn, her eldest brother, or Teddy, as he was affectionately called, had passed to his rest. This event, coupled with her already compromised cognitive situation became the trigger, I believe, for the rapid decent that followed.

It was now that I began to learn about the phenomenon known as "Sundowning," only to discover that some of the symptoms were evidenced in her behavior. An article from the AARP on Caregiving describes the Sundown Syndrome symptoms as follows:

"If your loved one has Alzheimer's disease or dementia, you may be seeing changes in their behavior in the late afternoon or early evening — a phenomenon known as sundown syndrome, sundowners or sundowning.

Research indicates that as many as 20 percent of people with Alzheimer's experience sundown syndrome, according to the Alzheimer's Association. With this symptom of dementia (and some other conditions, as well), the approach of sundown can trigger sudden emotional, behavioral or cognitive changes. These might include:

1. *mood swings*
2. *anxiety*
3. *sadness*
4. *restlessness*
5. *energy surges*
6. *increased confusion*
7. *hallucinations*
8. *delusions*

These may lead in turn to challenging behaviors like pacing, rocking, screaming, crying, disorientation, resistance, anger, aggression — or even violence. Many people experiencing sundown syndrome feel the urgent need to go somewhere or do something, but they can't always explain why." [1]

So, amid increasing anxiety, we began moving from lab tests to image scans, electronic sleep tests, etc. Each one returned no definitive sign of abnormalities, but she continued to decline. The attending Neurologist eventually diagnosed that Shirnet was experiencing early-onset dementia, and since there was no known cure, she would have to be on medications that are known only to slow the pace of decline. We embarked on the suggested medical regimen, accepting that the course of our lives was at this point forever changed.

SO, WHAT REALLY CHANGED?

The simple answer is that everything changed! Our plans were to retire and then revisit some of the places to which we traveled for work but never had time to really enjoy as the tourists do, spend time to bond with our grandchildren, develop the Charitable Foundation I helped to establish, and volunteer our time to serve the church wherever and whenever we could.

Much of that had to be placed on the back burner, as attending this great family emergency would now become priority number one. My role quickly transitioned from simply being a good "husband" to precipitously falling into the role of "full-time caregiver." This became a whole new area of learning and understanding for which I had to seek the requisite knowledge. This new phase of life was never part of any curriculum I had studied to date, except, as I recall, an experience I had early in life. It was in 1966 when as a 20-year-old youngster, I made my first trip to Toronto, Canada in search of educational and other opportunities in life. I secured employment at a Nursing home in Etobicoke, where people of advanced age were cared for, but among them were some who were afflicted with what I now realize was Dementia and Alzheimer's disease. Then, those names meant nothing, just another problem that required me to restrain to bed those troublesome ones who would go around to disturb other patients. Many of the things they did or said I found really funny, and would even elicit some of those responses. But, this time, it was not a joking matter. I was in it for real and would not be going home leaving the patients at 5:00 pm. It was going to be 24x7.

I began to reflect on the good times we had and our life together for almost 50 years. How would life be with our not being able to interact in any meaningful way? How long would this be? Will I be able to cope and give her the care she deserves? Questions like an endless stream kept coursing through my mind, and no one was able to answer them.

She had by now deteriorated to the point that adjustments had to be made with the shower stall, adding hand bars, shower seats, and toilet seats, and walking was not possible unaided so we had to get a wheelchair. Going up and down the stairs was stressful, to the point she actually fell and cracked a pelvic bone, further complicating our lives. We then decided to get a stairlift installed to transport her up and down to avoid further slipping and falling. Personal care was nonexistent, so I had to take that on in addition to meal preparation and house maintenance.

The crowning act, which was more painful than anything I ever emotionally experienced, was the night she looked at me in the bed, and asked, **"Who are you, and what are you doing in this bed?"** I was really at the point of tears.

Thank God for family, as soon we had in-laws, cousins, and brothers coming in to spend extended periods in order to help and offer support. It was truly a great relief and greatly appreciated to have them all during this time of confusion and stress. There were a few friends from our local congregation who would come over to ensure she was properly and appropriately dressed for Church whenever family members were no longer available. We had to use the wheelchair to Church, to the Doctor's appointments, to the therapy sessions, and sometimes upon returning home, she would refuse to exit the car, saying this was not her house! We had to coax her out by using different strategies; it was not easy to manage.

THE TURN AROUND

Since I was well aware that there was no known cure for her situation, I was willing to try as many worthwhile suggestions as I thought might hold without hurting! In addition to prescribed medications, we added Rosemary Tea, cold-pressed coconut oil, and much prayer. In the presence of family members, our Pastor conducted an anointing and prayer service in our home. Another idea developed to take a trip back to Jamaica and visit familiar places and friends, with the hope that something cognitively might be triggered.

So, in December 2019, we set off to Jamaica to spend at least a month. This proved to be a good decision. As she met family members and began to reminisce on old times and experiences, her recall was greatly stimulated. Similar reactions were evident when we visited familiar places, chief among which was the campsite where we first met and the Puerto Seco beach where we swam and chatted. Though it was a slow process, some incremental progress was beginning to appear. We tried to have as good a vacation as we could. When we were ready to return, although she needed a wheelchair to go to Jamaica, movement was easier during the return.

It was to the shocking delight of the church members when, instead of being in a wheelchair like the last time we worshipped together, Shirnet was now walking side by side, hand in hand with me to our usual seat. There was a spontaneous "Amen, Praise the Lord" coming from those who noticed. The memory situation continued to progress, to the point she now recognized she was ill and wanted to know from me what had happened.

I could not tell the full story at once, for in any case, she would not recall that much, so I served it in small doses! She could, by this time, resume some personal care matters, light domestic activities, and engage in conversations. The aspect of memory that plagues her, even now, is her inability to recall recent conversations, and will still repeat questions, needing to know the time of day, month, and year. While she still makes the effort to recall, it does not happen all the time. Well, she's at the place where many people who do not have her diagnosis are having problems with the recall. If this is as much healing as we can receive from our efforts and our prayers, we continue to give everlasting praise to God for restoration thus far. I can confidently declare, you dear reader, that, ***"It is no secret what God can do; what He's done for others, He'll do for you!"***

AFTERWORD

We as a family continue to happily live with our miracle, as I am not aware of anyone before this who has gone this far and returned to this level of cognition and function. Today, we travel to different places and countries, not as much as we used to, but sufficiently as retirees to enjoy what we still can of life.

I want to use this opportunity to thank all who have contributed in any way to making the journey easier for us; whether it was through your physical presence, your calls, or your prayers. Neither Rohann, Handel, nor myself have the ability to repay you for such generosity of self as you have shown, but I know someone who can, and I have already made the petition on your behalf. The Eternal God will prosper your outgoings and your incomings, and satisfy you with good health and abundance of blessings.

As I draw this narrative to a close, I am filled with gratitude for the opportunity to share my journey with you. Through the pages of "My Journey of Challenge, Faith, and Triumph," I have bared my soul, recounting the highs and lows, the struggles and victories that have shaped me into the person I am today. Truly, it has been quite a ride! It is my sincere hope that in reading my story, you have found inspiration and strength to face your own challenges with unwavering faith. May my experiences serve as a beacon of hope, reminding you that with faith and perseverance, even the most daunting obstacles can be overcome. As you close this book and continue your own journey, remember that each trial is an opportunity for growth and each triumph a testament to the power of belief, especially in a God who cares. Thank you for joining me on this remarkable odyssey; may your path be illuminated by the light of faith and guided by the wisdom of experience.

Shirnet and Leon taking a cruise on the Caribbean Princess

Handel, Carmen, Charles and Cataleya

Rohann, Lisa, Ariel and Jaxon

Valnie & Ivorine Wellington & Leon & Shirnet Wellington celebrating 50th and 52nd Wedding Anniversary in December 2023

Parents with Carmen Wellington

NOTES

ABOUT THE AUTHOR

1. *Wikipedia- History of Jamaica.* Donny L. Hamilton 2000, The Port Royal Project, World Wide Web, URL, http://nautarch.tamu.edu/portroyal/, Nautical Archaeology Program, Texas A&M University For additional details, contact Donny L. Hamilton (dlhamilton@tamu.edu).

1. BACK TO BASICS

1. babylist.com via Drugs.com portal
2. Source: Musixmatch

4. WEST INDIES UNION CONFERENCE

1. https://cdm.llu.edu/digital/collection/amhpa

5. GENERAL CONFERENCE OF SEVENTH-DAY ADVENTISTS

1. https://www.adventist.org/church/world-church/general-conference/
2. Balvin B Braham, A Practical Guide to Evangelism, pp 49-50.
3. https://www.adventist.org/church/world-church/inter-american/

6. REALITY CHECK

1. https://www.aarp.org/caregiving/health/info-2017/ways-to-manage-sundown-syndrome.html?CMP=KNC-DSO-CAREGIVING-Caregiving-SundownSyndrome-10625-GOOG-SundownSyndrome-Exact-NonBrand-ENG&ds_rl=1288354&gclid=Cj0KCQjwnJaKBhDgARIsAHmvz6fduJbfl4y8jhPKCP9EMI8JsAkti

A64QqF8QBQEhqPSQmSiblv0nq0aAldiEALw_wcB&gclsrc=
aw.ds

www.ingramcontent.com/pod-product-compliance
Lightning Source LLC
Chambersburg PA
CBHW040953110726
48007CB00001B/1